Windows Vista™
Top 100

Simplified®
TIPS & TRICKS

by Paul McFedries

Visual™

1807
WILEY
2007

Wiley Publishing, Inc.

Windows Vista™: Top 100 Simplified® Tips & Tricks

Published by
Wiley Publishing, Inc.
111 River Street
Hoboken, NJ 07030-5774

Published simultaneously in Canada

Copyright © 2007 by Wiley Publishing, Inc., Indianapolis, Indiana

Library of Congress Control Number: 2006934803

ISBN-13: 978-0-470-04574-9
ISBN-10: 0-470-04574-4
Manufactured in the United States of America

10 9 8 7 6 5 4 3 2 1
1K/QZ/RR/QW/IN

Trademark Acknowledgments

Contact Us

For general information on our other products and services contact our Customer Care Department within the U.S. at 800-762-2974, outside the U.S. at 317-572-3993, or fax 317-572-4002.

For technical support please visit www.wiley.com/techsupport.

WILEY
Wiley Publishing, Inc.

Sales

Contact Wiley at (800) 762-2974 or fax (317) 572-4002.

PRAISE FOR VISUAL BOOKS

"I have to praise you and your company on the fine products you turn out. I have twelve Visual books in my house. They were instrumental in helping me pass a difficult computer course. Thank you for creating books that are easy to follow. Keep turning out those quality books."

Gordon Justin (Brielle, NJ)

"What fantastic teaching books you have produced! Congratulations to you and your staff. You deserve the Nobel prize in Education. Thanks for helping me understand computers."

Bruno Tonon (Melbourne, Australia)

"A Picture Is Worth A Thousand Words! If your learning method is by observing or hands-on training, this is the book for you!"

Lorri Pegan-Durastante (Wickliffe, OH)

"Over time, I have bought a number of your 'Read Less - Learn More' books. For me, they are THE way to learn anything easily. I learn easiest using your method of teaching."

José A. Mazón (Cuba, NY)

"You've got a fan for life!! Thanks so much!!"

Kevin P. Quinn (Oakland, CA)

"I have several books from the Visual series and have always found them to be valuable resources."

Stephen P. Miller (Ballston Spa, NY)

"I have several of your Visual books and they are the best I have ever used."

Stanley Clark (Crawfordville, FL)

"Like a lot of other people, I understand things best when I see them visually. Your books really make learning easy and life more fun."

John T. Frey (Cadillac, MI)

"I have quite a few of your Visual books and have been very pleased with all of them. I love the way the lessons are presented!"

Mary Jane Newman (Yorba Linda, CA)

"Thank you, thank you, thank you...for making it so easy for me to break into this high-tech world."

Gay O'Donnell (Calgary, Alberta, Canada)

"I write to extend my thanks and appreciation for your books. They are clear, easy to follow, and straight to the point. Keep up the good work! I bought several of your books and they are just right! No regrets! I will always buy your books because they are the best."

Seward Kollie (Dakar, Senegal)

"I would like to take this time to thank you and your company for producing great and easy-to-learn products. I bought two of your books from a local bookstore, and it was the best investment I've ever made! Thank you for thinking of us ordinary people."

Jeff Eastman (West Des Moines, IA)

"Compliments to the chef!! Your books are extraordinary! Or, simply put, extra-ordinary, meaning way above the rest! THANKYOU THANKYOU THANKYOU! I buy them for friends, family, and colleagues."

Christine J. Manfrin (Castle Rock, CO)

CREDITS

Project Editor
Jade L. Williams

Acquisitions Editor
Jody Lefevere

Product Development Supervisor
Courtney Allen

Copy Editor
Jerelind Charles

Technical Editor
Lee Musick

Editorial Manager
Robyn Siesky

Business Manager
Amy Knies

Editorial Assistant
Laura Sinise

Manufacturing
Allan Conley
Linda Cook
Paul Gilchrist
Jennifer Guynn

Book Design
Kathie Rickard

Production Coordinator
Jennifer Theriot

Layout
Beth Brooks
Jennifer Mayberry
Amanda Spagnuolo

Screen Artist
Jill A. Proll

Proofreader
Mildred Rosenzweig

Indexer
Stephen Ingle

Quality Control
John Greenough
Brian H. Walls

Cover Design
Anthony Bunyan

Vice President and Executive Group Publisher
Richard Swadley

Vice President and Publisher
Barry Pruett

Composition Director
Debbie Stailey

ABOUT THE AUTHOR

Paul McFedries is the president of Logophilia Limited, a technical writing company. While now primarily a writer, Paul has worked as a programmer, consultant, and Web site developer. Paul has written nearly 50 books that have sold more than three million copies worldwide. These books include the Wiley titles *Windows XP: Top 100 Simplified Tips and Tricks, Second Edition* and *Teach Yourself VISUALLY Computers, Fourth Edition*. Paul also runs Word Spy, a Web site dedicated to tracking new words and phrases (see www.wordspy.com).

HOW TO USE THIS BOOK

Windows Vista: Top 100 Simplified Tips & Tricks includes 100 tasks that reveal cool secrets, teach timesaving tricks, and explain great tips guaranteed to make you more productive with Windows Vista. The easy-to-use layout lets you work through all the tasks from beginning to end or jump in at random.

Who is this book for?

You already know Windows Vista basics. Now you'd like to go beyond, with shortcuts, tricks, and tips that let you work smarter and faster. And because you learn more easily when someone *shows* you how, this is the book for you.

Conventions Used In This Book

❶ Steps

This book uses step-by-step instructions to guide you easily through each task. Numbered callouts on every screen shot show you exactly how to perform each task, step by step.

❷ Tips

Practical tips provide insights to save you time and trouble, caution you about hazards to avoid, and reveal how to do things in Windows Vista that you never thought possible!

❸ Task Numbers

Task numbers from 1 to 100 indicate which lesson you are working on.

❹ Difficulty Levels

For quick reference, the symbols below mark the difficulty level of each task.

DIFFICULTY LEVEL — Demonstrates a new spin on a common task

DIFFICULTY LEVEL — Introduces a new skill or a new task

DIFFICULTY LEVEL — Combines multiple skills requiring in-depth knowledge

DIFFICULTY LEVEL — Requires extensive skill and may involve other technologies

In order to get this information to you in a timely manner, this book was based on a pre-release version of Microsoft Vista 2007/Microsoft Office 2007. There may be some minor changes between the screenshots in this book and what you see on your desktop. As always, Microsoft has the final word on how programs look and function; if you have any questions or see any discrepancies, consult the online help for further information about the software.

Table of Contents

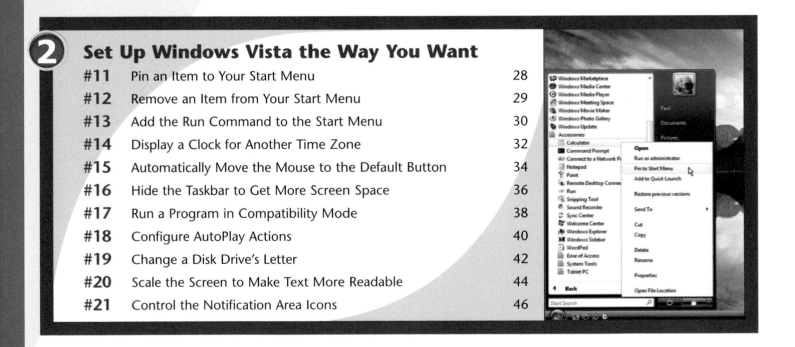

Table of Contents

7 Make E-Mail Easier

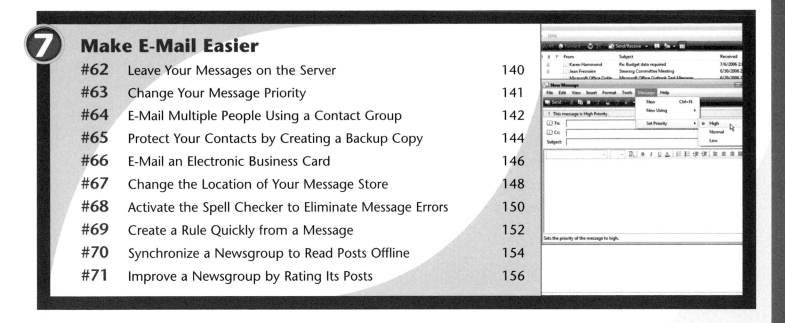

8 Enhance Your Computer's Security and Privacy

Table of Contents

Make Windows Vista Faster and More Efficient

Whether you use Windows Vista at work or at home, you probably want to spend your computer time creating documents, sending and receiving e-mail, browsing the Web, playing games, and doing other useful and fun activities. You probably do *not* want to spend your time wrestling with Windows Vista or waiting for it to finish its tasks.

Using a few simple techniques, you can make working with Windows Vista faster and more convenient. For example, rather than opening a number of Start menu folders to get to a program, you can create a shortcut in a more convenient location.

Also, you can work with a few settings to ensure Windows Vista is working quickly and

efficiently. For example, you can speed up your display by reducing the number of visual effects Windows Vista uses to draw screen elements.

Sometimes getting the most out of Windows Vista is a simple matter of taking care of the little details. For example, do you find yourself wasting precious time every time you accidentally press the Caps Lock key and have to delete and retype the errant text? If so, you can avoid the problem altogether by setting up Windows Vista to warn you when you turn on Caps Lock.

This chapter introduces you to these and many other techniques for maximizing your Windows Vista productivity.

Top 100

CREATE SHORTCUTS
for your favorite programs

If you have a program that you use regularly, you can access the program more quickly by creating a shortcut. A *shortcut* is a special file that points to a program. When you double-click the shortcut, Windows Vista automatically loads that program.

Shortcuts become particularly handy when you create them in a convenient location. For example, you can create a program shortcut on your Windows Vista desktop. That way, instead of clicking the Start

menu and opening a number of subfolders to find and launch a particular program, you can simply double-click the shortcut on the desktop.

You can create as many shortcuts as you want; the Windows Vista desktop offers a number of features that help you keep your shortcuts organized. And if you find that you no longer use a shortcut, you can safely delete it without affecting the associated program.

① Right-click the location on your desktop where you want to create the shortcut.

② Click New.

③ Click Shortcut.

The Create Shortcut wizard appears.

④ Click Browse.

The Browse for Files or Folders dialog box appears.

⑤ Select the program that you want the shortcut to start.

Note: *You can also create shortcuts to documents.*

⑥ Click OK.

⑦ Click Next.

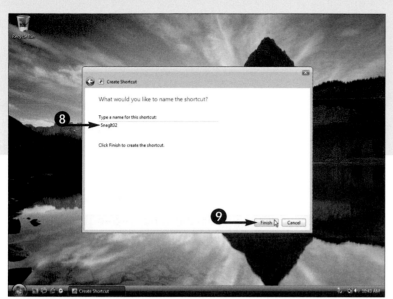

8 Type a name for the shortcut.

9 Click Finish.

DIFFICULTY LEVEL

● An icon for the shortcut appears on the desktop.

Note: You can also pin shortcuts to your Start menu, as explained in Task #11.

TIPS

Taskbar Trick!

The problem with adding shortcuts to your desktop is that other windows often obscure the desktop, particularly if you prefer running your program windows maximized. However, Windows gives you a quick method to get to the desktop. Right-click an empty section of the taskbar and then click Show the Desktop.

Desktop Trick!

If you frequently use the Windows Vista desktop to store your program shortcuts, the desktop can quickly become a jumble of icons that make it difficult to find the shortcut you want. To solve this problem, right-click an empty spot on the desktop, click Sort By and then click Name. This sorts the shortcuts alphabetically by name.

ADJUST VISUAL EFFECTS
for best performance

You can turn off some or all of the visual effects that Windows Vista uses to display screen elements. This reduces the load on your computer, which improves the overall performance of your machine.

These visual effects include the animation Windows Vista uses when you minimize or maximize a window. For example, when you minimize a window, it appears to shrink down to the taskbar. Such effects are designed to help a novice user better understand what is happening on their computer.

For graphics in general, and the visual effects in particular, performance is mostly determined by the

amount of memory on the *graphics adapter*. This is a circuit board inside your computer that processes the graphical data generated by Windows Vista and displayed on your monitor. The more memory on the adapter, the faster it can process the visual effects.

Most new computers have a decent amount of adapter memory — at least 32MB — so turning off visual effects will have little impact on performance. If your adapter has 8MB or less, turning off visual effects can improve performance.

① Click Start.

② Right-click Computer.

③ Click Properties.

The System window appears.

④ Click Advanced System Settings.

Note: If the User Account Control dialog box appears, click Continue or type an administrator password and click Submit.

The System Properties dialog box appears.

⑤ Click the Advanced tab.

⑥ In the Performance area, click Settings.

The Performance Options dialog box appears.

⑦ Click the Adjust for best performance option (○ changes to ◉).

⑧ Click OK to return to the System Properties dialog box.

Windows Vista turns off the visual effects.

DIFFICULTY LEVEL

⑨ Click OK.

The System Properties dialog box closes.

⑩ Click the Close box.

TIPS

Customize It!

If you prefer to turn off only certain visual effects, click the Adjust for best appearance option in step **7** (○ changes to ◉) to ensure all the effects are activated. Click the Custom option (○ changes to ◉) and then click the check box for each visual effect you want to turn off (☑ changes to ☐).

Did You Know?

If you do not know how much memory your graphics adapter has, Windows Vista can tell you. Follow steps **1** to **3** to display the System window, and then click the Windows Experience Index link. In the Performance Information and Tools window that appears, click the View and print details link. The Dedicated graphics memory value tells you the amount of memory in your graphics adapter.

Ensure Windows Vista is
OPTIMIZED FOR PROGRAMS

You can set an option that ensures Windows Vista maximizes the performance of your programs. This option controls processor scheduling in Windows Vista.

The *processor* (or *CPU*) is the chip inside your machine that coordinates all the computer's activity; some call it the brain of the computer. *Processor scheduling* determines how much time the processor allocates to the computer's activities. In particular, processor scheduling differentiates between the *foreground program* — the program in which you are

currently working — and *background programs* — programs that perform tasks, such as printing or backing up, while you work in another program.

Memory (or *RAM*) is a set of chips inside your computer that constitute the work area of the machine. Programs and files are loaded from the hard drive into memory. Windows Vista sets aside a portion of memory as the *system cache*, which holds recently used data for faster access. In terms of *memory usage*, the bigger the system cache, the less memory is available for your programs, which can reduce performance.

❶ Click Start.

❷ Right-click Computer.

❸ Click Properties.

The System window appears.

❹ Click Advanced System Settings.

Note: *If the User Account Control dialog box appears, click Continue or type an administrator password and click Submit.*

The System Properties dialog box appears.

❺ Click the Advanced tab.

❻ In the Performance area, click Settings.

3

DIFFICULTY LEVEL

The Performance Options dialog box appears.

⑦ Click the Advanced tab.

⑧ In the Processor scheduling area, click the Programs option (○ changes to ◉).

⑨ Click OK to return to the System Properties dialog box.

Windows Vista applies the performance settings.

⑩ Click OK.

⑪ Click the Close box.

The System Properties dialog box closes.

 TIPS

Did You Know?

There are circumstances where you may be better off clicking the Background services option (○ changes to ◉) in the Advanced tab of the Performance Options dialog box. Specifically, if you often use programs that typically perform a great deal of work in the background, you can benefit from this choice. Good examples are the Windows Vista Backup program and Windows Update, both of which perform processor-intensive tasks in the background, and so would perform faster if given more processor cycles.

Did You Know?

If you do not know what kind of processor or how much memory your computer has, Windows Vista can tell you. Follow steps **1** to **3** to display the System window and then click the Windows Experience Index link. In the Performance Information and Tools window that appears, click the View and print details link. In the Details column, read the Processor and Memory (RAM) values. See Task #10 to learn how to determine your system rating.

IMPROVE PERFORMANCE
with a USB flash drive

If you add a USB flash drive to your computer, Windows Vista can use the memory on that drive to improve the performance of your system. Windows Vista uses a technology named SuperFetch to boost system performance. SuperFetch tracks the programs and data you use over time to create a kind of profile of your hard drive usage. Using this profile, SuperFetch can then anticipate the data that you might use in the near future. It would then load (fetch) that data into memory ahead of time. If that data was indeed what your system required, then performance would increase because Vista would not have to retrieve the data from your hard drive.

However, SuperFetch goes even further by also using Vista's new ReadyBoost technology. If you insert a USB 2.0 flash drive (also called a memory key) into your system, Windows Vista asks you if you want to use the device to speed up your system. If you elect to do this, SuperFetch will use that drive's capacity as storage for the data that SuperFetch anticipates you will require. This frees up the system memory that SuperFetch would otherwise use for storage, and more available memory means better performance for Windows Vista and your programs.

SPEED UP YOUR SYSTEM WITH FLASH DRIVE MEMORY

① Insert a flash drive into a USB port on your computer.

The AutoPlay dialog box appears.

② Click the Speed up my system option.

Windows Vista configures SuperFetch to use the flash drive's memory.

CONFIGURE THE AMOUNT OF FLASH DRIVE MEMORY USED BY WINDOWS

① Click Start.

② Click Computer.

#4

DIFFICULTY LEVEL

The Computer window appears.

③ Click the flash drive icon.

④ Click Properties.

The drive's Properties dialog box appears.

⑤ Click the ReadyBoost tab.

⑥ Click and drag the slider to set the amount of drive memory Vista sets aside for SuperFetch.

⑦ Click OK.

TIPS

Did You Know?

If you have two USB flash drives and your computer has two available USB ports, you can insert both flash drives and tell Windows Vista to use them both to speed up your system. You should also know that you probably will not see much improvement in performance if your system has at least 1GB of RAM, because SuperFetch does not need extra space when it has that much memory available.

Reverse It!

If you decide later on that you want to use the flash drive's full capacity for file storage, you can tell Windows Vista not to use the drive to augment SuperFetch. Click Start, Computer, click the flash drive, and then click Properties. Click the ReadyBoost tab and then click the Do not use this device option (○ changes to ⦿). Click OK to put the new setting into effect.

Run a program with
ELEVATED PRIVILEGES

If you need to perform advanced tasks in a program, you may need to run that program with elevated privileges.

Windows Vista implements a new security model named *user account control* (UAC). The basic idea behind this new security strategy is that you have permission to perform only a few day-to-day Windows tasks, such as moving and copying files. For more ambitious tasks that could affect the security of the system, Windows Vista asks you to provide credentials to prove that the task is not being performed by a virus program or other malicious software.

The credentials you provide depend on the type of account you have. If you have an administrator

account, you click Continue in the User Account Control dialog box; if you have a standard user account, you have to provide an administrator password.

However, this security model falls short when you need to perform certain actions. For example, if you edit a file in one of the Windows Vista protected folders, you will receive a Permission Denied error when you try to save your changes.

To work around such problems, you need to start the program you are using with elevated privileges. This tells Vista to run the program as though you were using the Administrator account, the highest-level account on your system, and the only account that does not need to provide credentials.

① Click Start.

② Click All Programs.

③ Open the Start menu folder that contains the icon of the program you want to run.

● For example, to run the Command Prompt with elevated privileges, click Accessories.

④ Right-click the program icon (for example, the Command Prompt icon).

⑤ Click Run as administrator.

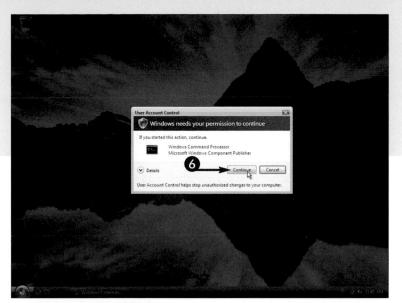

The User Account Control dialog box appears.

6 Click Continue.

If you have a standard user account, type the password for an administrator and then click Submit, instead.

Windows Vista runs the program with elevated privileges.

TIPS

Did You Know?

If you have a program that you use frequently and you normally run it with elevated privileges, you can tell Windows Vista to always run the program elevated. Follow steps **1** to **3** in this task to find the program icon, right-click the icon, and then click Properties. Click the Compatibility tab, click the Run this program as an administrator check box (☐ changes to ☑), and then click OK.

Caution!

When you run a program with elevated privileges, it not only enables you to perform otherwise forbidden tasks using the program, but the program itself can perform tasks that programs are usually prevented from doing (at least until you enter your credentials to allow them access to the system). Because elevated programs can perform forbidden tasks, only elevate privileges for programs you know and trust. Otherwise, you might inadvertently give a virus or Trojan horse program complete access to your system.

Make your file searches
RUN FASTER

You can add folders to the Windows Search engine's index, which makes your file searches in those folders run noticeably faster.

Having a lot of data is certainly not a bad thing, but *finding* the file you want among all that data can get frustrating. Fortunately, the Windows Vista Search feature can help by enabling you to search for files based on name, content, size, and more.

This works well if what you are looking for is in your main user account folder or one of its subfolders (such as Documents, Pictures, and Music). This is

because Windows Vista automatically *indexes* those folders, which means it keeps a detailed record of the contents of all your files. Using this index, the Search feature can find files up to a hundred times faster than without an index.

However, if you have files in a different location, Windows Vista does not index them, so searching those files is very time-consuming. You can dramatically speed up the searching of those files by adding their location to the Search index.

① Click Start.

② Click Control Panel.

The Control Panel window appears.

③ Click System and Maintenance.

The System and Maintenance window appears.

④ Click Indexing Options.

The Indexing Options dialog box appears.

5 Click Modify.

#6

DIFFICULTY LEVEL

6 Show all locations.

Note: If the User Account Control dialog box appears, click Continue or type an administrator password and click Submit.

The Indexed Locations dialog box appears.

7 Click the folder you want to include in the index.

● The folder appears in the list of included locations.

8 Click OK.

9 Click Close.

Windows Vista includes the folder in the index and begins rebuilding the index.

Note: See Task #36 to learn how to run advanced searches in Windows Vista.

TIPS

Did You Know?

If Windows Vista takes a long time to search or cannot find your files, you may need to rebuild the index. Follow steps **1** to **5** to display the Indexing Options dialog box and activate the global settings. Click Advanced to display the Advanced Options dialog box, and then click Rebuild.

Caution!

The catalog created by the Indexing Service can use up hundreds of megabytes of hard drive space. To move the catalog to a hard drive with more space, follow steps **1** to **5** to display the Indexing Options dialog box and activate the global settings. Click Advanced to display the Advanced Options dialog box. Click Move, select a new location, and then click OK.

HEAR AN ALERT
when you press the Caps Lock key

You can adjust a setting that tells Windows Vista to beep your computer's speaker whenever you press the Caps Lock key.

When you are typing quickly, it is common to accidentally press the Caps Lock key instead of either Shift, Tab, or A. As you probably know, when you inadvertently press Caps Lock, it may be a while before you realize it. This means that you end up with a great deal of typing that has the capital letters reversed. Not only must you delete this text, but you must also retype it with the correct letters, all of which wastes valuable time.

To save all the time it takes to fix mistakes caused by accidentally pressing Caps Lock, you can configure Windows Vista to beep your computer's speaker when you press Caps Lock. This alerts you that Caps Lock is now activated, so you can immediately press the key again to deactivate it and continue with your work after only a short interruption. It is also possible to quickly disable the Caps Lock alert for those times when you need to use the Caps Lock feature.

1 Click Start.

2 Click Control Panel.

The Control Panel window appears.

3 Click Ease of Access.

The Ease of Access Center window appears.

④ Click Change how your keyboard works.

DIFFICULTY LEVEL

⑤ Click the Turn on Toggle Keys check box (☐ changes to ☑).

⑥ Click Save.

⑦ Click the Close box to close the Ease of Access Center window.

Windows alerts you with a tone when you press the Caps Lock key.

Did You Know?

You can turn off Toggle Keys by holding down the Num Lock key for five seconds, until you hear a beep. To turn it back on, hold down Num Lock for five seconds, until you see the Toggle Keys dialog box. Click OK to turn Toggle Keys on; click Cancel to leave Toggle Keys off.

Did You Know?

Many of today's keyboards come with settings that enable you to disable Caps Lock. To check for such a setting, click Start, Control Panel, Hardware and Sound, and then Keyboard to display the Keyboard Properties dialog box. Look for a tab named Key Settings or something similar and then look for a Caps Lock option that you can turn off.

DISPLAY MORE PROGRAMS
on your Start menu

You can customize the Start menu to display more of the programs you use most often.

The list displaying your most-frequently used programs appears on the bottom-left side of the Start menu, above All Programs. As you work with your programs, Windows Vista keeps track of how many times you launch each one. The programs that you have launched most often appear on the Start menu for easy, two-click access. These programs appear at the top of the list, followed by the next

most-often-used programs, and so on. When another program becomes popular, Windows Vista drops the bottom program and adds the new one.

Unfortunately, the default Start menu shows just the six most popular programs. If you find that some of your regular programs are constantly getting dropped from the Start menu, you can increase the size of the list to force Windows Vista to display more programs.

❶ Right-click Start.

❷ Click Properties.

The Taskbar and Start Menu Properties dialog box appears.

❸ Click the Start Menu tab.

❹ Click Customize.

The Customize Start Menu dialog box appears.

⑤ Type the number of programs you want to see.

Note: The maximum number of programs is 30.

⑥ Click OK to return to the Taskbar and Start Menu Properties dialog box.

⑦ Click OK.

● Windows Vista adjusts the size of the Start menu's most-frequently used program list.

TIPS

More Options!

The height of the Start menu is restricted by the height of your screen. To display more Start menu items without changing the screen height, follow steps **1** to **4** to open the Customize Start Menu dialog box. In the list, click to uncheck the Use large icons check box (☑ changes to ☐), and then click OK. Using smaller icons enables more items to appear on the Start menu.

Customize It!

If you want to get even more items on the Start menu, you can change the height of your screen by increasing the screen resolution. Right-click the desktop, click Personalize, and then click Display Settings. In the Display Settings dialog box, click and drag the Resolution slider to the right, and then click OK.

LAUNCH CONTROL PANEL ICONS
faster by using a menu

You can quickly access items in the Control Panel by converting the Start menu's Control Panel item into a menu.

Control Panel is the Windows Vista customization shop, with more than 50 icons. Using these icons, you can customize and modify features such as accessibility, the display, folders and fonts, the Internet, and user accounts. You can install and uninstall programs and devices, and you can tweak specific devices such as game controllers, the keyboard, the mouse, the modem, printers, scanners, and more.

The longer you use Windows Vista, the more you appreciate the Control Panel. The problem, however, is that the default Control Panel window uses a category view that groups the Control Panel icons into categories, such as System and Maintenance, Security, and Appearance and Personalization. That view hampers more experienced users, who must often negotiate several windows to get to the icon they want. Converting the Start menu's Control Panel item into a menu on the Start menu enables you to easily find and choose any Control Panel item.

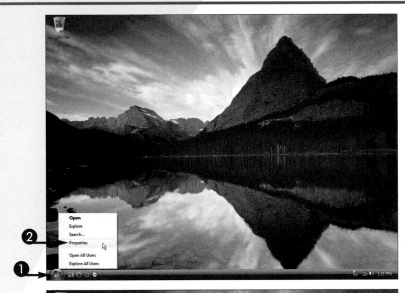

❶ Right-click Start.

❷ Click Properties.

The Taskbar and Start Menu Properties dialog box appears.

❸ Click the Start Menu tab.

❹ Click Customize.

The Customize Start Menu dialog box appears.

5 In the list of Start menu items, under Control Panel, click the Display as a menu option (○ changes to ◉).

6 Click OK to return to the Taskbar and Start Menu Properties dialog box.

7 Click OK.

8 Click Start.

9 Click Control Panel.

● A menu of the Control Panel items appears.

● If the entire menu does not fit on your screen, position the mouse here to expand the menu.

TIPS

More Options!

There are other Start menu items that you can display as menus. Follow steps **1** to **5** to display the Customize Start Menu dialog box. The following branches have a Display as a menu option that you can click (○ changes to ◉): Computer, Documents, Games, Music, Personal folder, and Pictures.

More Options!

For easier access to some of your documents, follow steps **1** to **5** to display the Customize Start Menu dialog box. Click the Favorites menu check box (☐ changes to ☑) to display a menu of Internet Explorer favorites. Click OK to return to the Start menu tab. Click the Store and display a list of recently opened files check box (☐ changes to ☑) to display a list of the 15 documents you have used most recently.

UPDATE A DEVICE DRIVER
to ensure top device performance

You can ensure that a device is working at optimum performance by updating the device's driver to the latest version.

Windows Vista acts as a go-between for you and your programs and the hardware devices on your system. For example, when you press a key on your keyboard, Windows Vista accepts the keystroke and either displays it on screen (if you are typing) or runs a command (if you pressed a shortcut key).

Windows Vista communicates with a hardware device by using a small program called a *device driver*, and

this communication works two ways: from the device and to the device. For example, a keyboard uses its device driver to let Windows Vista know which key you pressed.

Hardware manufacturers often create new versions of their device drivers to fix problems and improve the device's performance. For these reasons, it is a good idea to always use the latest device drivers for your system's hardware. After you download a new driver from the manufacturer's Web site, you then need to update the existing driver on your system.

❶ Click Start.

❷ Click Control Panel.

The Control Panel window appears.

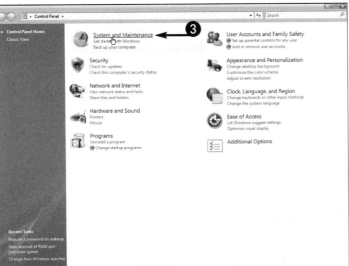

❸ Click System and Maintenance.

The System and Maintenance window appears.

4 Click Device Manager.

Note: If the User Account Control dialog box appears, click Continue or type an administrator password and click Submit.

DIFFICULTY LEVEL

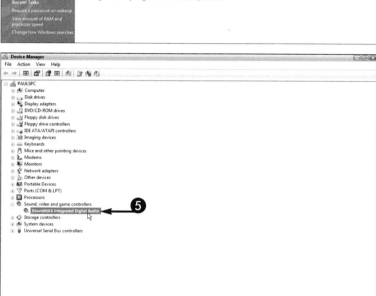

The Device Manager window appears.

5 Click the device you want to update.

TIPS

Check It Out!

Windows Vista has a new feature that enables you to quickly update the drivers of those devices that were not installed properly on your system. Click Start, All Programs, Accessories, Welcome Center, and then double-click Set up devices. (If you do not see this icon, click the Show all X items link.) If the User Account Control dialog box appears, click Continue or type an administrator password and click Submit.

Did You Know?

If you have a device that is performing slowly or is having problems, the cause may be a corrupted device driver file. In most cases, you can fix this problem by reinstalling the device's driver. Follow the steps in this task and, when it is time to select the driver, select the original driver, which is usually on the CD that came with the device.

UPDATE A DEVICE DRIVER
to ensure top device performance

Most device manufacturers offer a Web site where you can download the latest drivers, but it helps to know how to navigate these sites.

Look for an area of the site dedicated to driver downloads. The good sites have links to areas named Downloads or Drivers, but it is far more common to first have to go through a Support or Customer Service area.

Go through each step the site provides. For example, it is common to have to select an overall driver category, and then a device category, and then a line category, and then the specific model you have.

When you get to the device's download page, be careful which file you choose. Make sure that it is a Windows Vista driver, and make sure that you are not downloading a utility program or some other non-driver file.

When you finally get to download the file, save it to your computer. The best location is your user account's Downloads folder.

6 Click the Update Driver Software button.

The Update Driver Software dialog box appears.

7 Click Browse my computer for driver software.

Note: If you have a CD with the device driver, insert the disc and click Search automatically for updated driver software, instead.

The Browse for driver software on your computer dialog box appears.

8 Type the location of the folder where you saved the downloaded driver.

#10 CONTINUED

● Alternatively, click Browse, use the Browse for Folder dialog box to select the folder, and then click OK.

9 Click Next.

Windows Vista installs the driver.

10 Click Close.

11 Click the Close box to close Device Manager.

Windows Vista now uses the updated device driver.

TIPS

Reverse It!

The latest device drivers are usually the most stable and bug-free. However, you may occasionally find that updating a device driver causes problems. In that case, you need to *roll back* the driver to the previous version. Follow steps **1** to **4** to display Device Manager, and then double-click your device. Click the Driver tab and then click the Roll Back Driver button.

Remove It!

When you remove a device from your system, Windows Vista usually recognizes that the device is no longer part of the system and it uninstalls the device's driver. However, Windows Vista will sometimes not realize the device is gone and continue to load the driver. If this happens, follow steps **1** to **4** to display Device Manager, right-click the device, and then click Uninstall.

Set Up Windows Vista
the Way You Want

Windows Vista is endlessly customizable and offers many features that enable you to modify the look and feel of your system to suit your style and the way you work.

You probably already know how to customize aspects of the Windows Vista screen, such as the colors, fonts, desktop background, and screen resolution. These are useful techniques to know, to be sure, but Windows Vista offers a number of other techniques that put much more emphasis on what is practical. That is, although changing your screen colors might make Windows Vista more interesting, it does not help you get your work done any faster. However, a technique such as revamping your Start menu for easy access to your most-used programs can save you lots of mouse clicks and, ultimately, lots of time.

This chapter focuses on the practical aspects of customizing Windows Vista by showing you a number of techniques, most of which are designed to save you time and make Windows Vista more efficient. You begin with several techniques that make your Start menu much easier to deal with, including adding icons permanently, removing unneeded icons, and putting the Run command on the Start menu.

Other techniques in this chapter include displaying clocks for other time zones, adding program icons to the handy Quick Launch toolbar, hiding the taskbar to get more screen space, getting older programs to run in Windows Vista, configuring the Windows Vista default behavior when you insert CDs, and customizing the icons in the notification area.

Top 100

PIN AN ITEM
to your Start menu

You can customize the Windows Vista Start menu to give yourself quick access to the programs that you use most often.

The items on the main Start menu — including Computer, Internet, E-mail — are very handy because they require just two clicks to launch. To start up all your other programs, you must also click All Programs and then negotiate one or more submenus. For those programs you use most often, you can avoid this extra work by *pinning* their icons permanently to the main Start menu.

All pinned program items appear on the left side of the Start menu, in the top section where the Internet and E-mail icons reside. If you have pinned several programs and you find this section is getting too crowded, you can remove a pinned item by right-clicking the item and then clicking Unpin from the Start menu.

DIFFICULTY LEVEL

❶ Click Start.

❷ Click All Programs.

  Note: After you click All Programs, the name changes to Back.

❸ If necessary, open the submenu that contains the program you want to pin to the Start menu. For example, if the program is in the Accessories submenu, click Accessories.

❹ Right-click the program icon.

❺ Click Pin to Start Menu.

● Windows Vista adds the program to the main Start menu.

● You can also use the same technique to pin any of the often-used program items to the main Start menu.

REMOVE AN ITEM
from your Start menu

You can remove Start menu program items that you no longer use, reducing the clutter and allowing other often-used programs to appear.

The left side of the main Start menu is divided into two sections. The top part consists of menu items that remain in place, including the Internet and E-mail icons and any pinned program items. The bottom part consists of shortcuts to the eight programs that you have used most often, so these change as you use your computer. You can remove shortcuts for programs that you no longer use from

either section on the left side of the S... You can also delete items — including ... program items but also entire submenus — from the All Programs menu and its various submenus. To do this, click Start, All Programs, and then open the menu that contains the item you want to delete. Right-click the item and then click Delete. When Windows Vista asks you to confirm the deletion, click Yes.

① Click Start.

② Right-click the item you want to remove.

③ Click Remove from this list.

● Windows Vista removes the item from the Start menu.

Note: See Task #8 to learn how to show more programs on the Start menu.

ADD THE RUN COMMAND
to the Start menu

If you often use the Run dialog box to open programs, folders, and Web sites, you can make the dialog box much easier to launch by adding the Run command to the main Start menu.

The Run command opens the Run dialog box, which enables you to open many different types of files by typing the file's address. The Run command enables you to launch programs, folders, documents, Web sites, e-mail messages, Command Prompt commands, and more.

The Run dialog box is a very handy tool, but if you use it frequently, you will be disappointed to find out that Windows Vista buries the Run command in the Accessories menu (select Start, All Programs, Accessories, and then Run). This is very inconvenient and very time-consuming. However, you can fix this problem by customizing Windows Vista to display the Run command on the main Start menu. This enables you to open the Run dialog box with just a couple of mouse clicks.

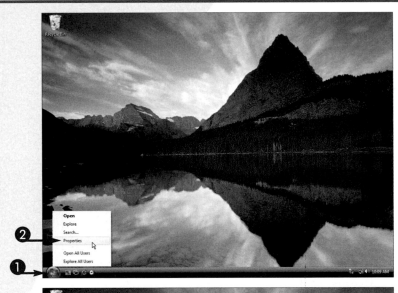

① Right-click the Start button.

② Click Properties.

The Taskbar and Start Menu Properties dialog box appears.

③ Click the Start Menu tab.

④ Click Customize.

The Customize Start Menu dialog box appears.

5 Click the Run command check box (☐ changes to ☑).

6 Click OK.

7 Click OK.

#**13**

DIFFICULTY LEVEL

8 Click Start.

● Windows Vista adds the Run command to the Start menu.

TIPS

Did You Know?
To start an e-mail message from the Run dialog box, type **mailto:** followed by the e-mail address of the recipient. For example, to start an e-mail message addressed to president@whitehouse.gov, type **mailto:president@whitehouse.gov** in the Run dialog box and then click OK.

Did You Know?
If your Windows Vista Start menu is already overcrowded, you might not want to add the Run command. One solution is to remove other Start menu items you do not use by following steps **1** to **4** and then deactivate the check boxes for the items you want to remove. Alternatively, leave Run off the main Start menu and launch the Run dialog box by pressing Windows Logo key+R.

Display a clock for
ANOTHER TIME ZONE

If you deal with people in another time zone, you can make it easier to find out the current time in that zone by customizing Windows Vista to show a second clock that is configured for the time zone.

If you have colleagues, friends, or family members who work or live in a different time zone, it is often important to know the correct time in that zone. For example, you would not want to call someone at home at 9 AM your time if that person lives in a time zone that is three hours behind you. Similarly, if you

know that a business colleague leaves work at 5 PM and that person works in a time zone that is seven hours ahead of you, then you know that any calls you place to that person must occur before 10 AM your time.

If you need to be sure about the current time in another time zone, you can customize the Windows Vista date and time display to show not only your current time, but also the current time in the other time zone.

1 Right-click the time.

2 Click Adjust Date/Time.

The Date and Time Properties dialog box appears.

3 Click the Additional Clocks tab.

4 Click the Show this clock check box (☐ changes to ☑).

5 Click here and then click the time zone you want to use in the new clock.

6 Type a name for the new clock.

7 Click OK.

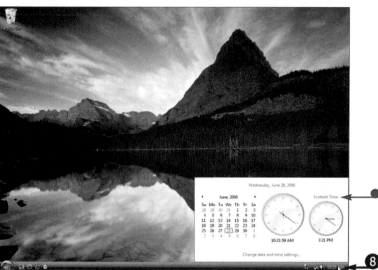

Windows Vista adds the clock.

8 Click the time.

● Windows Vista displays the extra clock.

TIPS

Did You Know?

After you customize Windows Vista with the extra clock, you normally click the time in the notification area to see both clocks. However, if you just hover the mouse pointer over the time, Windows Vista displays a banner that shows the current date, your current local time, and the current time in the other time zone.

More Options!

If you also deal with people in a third time zone, you can customize Windows Vista to display a third clock. Follow steps **1** to **3** to display the Additional Clocks tab. Click the second Show this clock check box (☐ changes to ☑), click the down arrow (▾) in the list below it to select a time zone, type a name for the third clock, and then click OK.

Automatically move the mouse to the
DEFAULT BUTTON

You can negotiate many dialog boxes much more quickly by customizing Windows Vista to automatically move the mouse pointer over the default dialog box button.

Most dialog boxes define a *default button*, which is most often the button that dismisses the dialog box and puts the dialog box settings into effect. The most common default dialog box button is the OK button.

Windows Vista makes it easy for you to find the default button by making the button glow while the dialog box is open. That is, the button's blue color gradually fades in and out.

Many dialog boxes do nothing more than provide you with information or a warning. In most of these cases, the only thing you need to do with the dialog box is click the default button. You can get past such dialog boxes much more quickly if you customize Windows Vista to automatically move the mouse pointer over the default button, because then all you have to do is click to dismiss the dialog box. If the dialog box requires more complex input from you, you still save time because the mouse pointer is already inside the dialog box.

1 Click Start.

2 Click Control Panel.

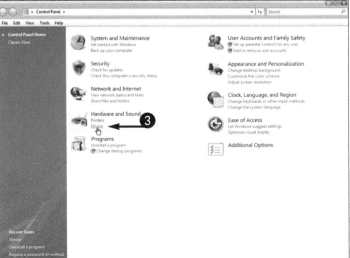

The Control Panel window appears.

3 Click Mouse.

The Mouse Properties dialog box appears.

④ Click the Pointer Options tab.

⑤ Click the Automatically move pointer to the default button in a dialog box check box (☐ changes to ☑).

⑥ Click OK.

Windows Vista automatically moves the mouse pointer to the default button each time you open a dialog box.

⑦ Click the Close box to close the Control Panel window.

Caution!

When the Snap To feature is activated, it is easy to get into the habit of quickly clicking whenever a notification dialog box appears. However, if you click too quickly, you may miss the message in the dialog box, which could be important. Remember to read all dialog box messages before clicking the default button.

More Options!

If you have excellent mouse control, another option that can save time in the long run is to increase the pointer speed, which enables you to get from one part of the screen to another much more quickly. Follow steps **1** to **5** to display the Pointer Options tab, click and drag the Select a pointer speed slider towards Fast, and then click OK.

Hide the taskbar to
GET MORE SCREEN SPACE

You can give yourself more vertical room on your screen by hiding the Windows Vista taskbar.

As you work with Windows Vista, you may find yourself wishing you had more room on your screen to display your programs. This is particularly true for people who do a lot of writing on their computer, because they often would like to see more of their text on the screen.

The most straightforward way to maximize the amount of room your program has on the screen is to maximize the program. You can also try turning off toolbars and other program features that you do not use.

Even if you do all of that, however, you still cannot use the maximum height of the screen because the Windows Vista taskbar takes up room on the bottom of the screen. Even when you maximize a program, the taskbar remains visible.

The taskbar is designed that way so that you always have access to it for switching programs. However, if you use a different method to switch programs, you may no longer require the taskbar to be visible at all times, so you can configure Windows Vista to hide it. This will give you maximized window full access to the screen.

① Right-click an empty section of the taskbar.

② Click Properties.

The Taskbar and Start Menu Properties dialog box appears.

③ Click the Taskbar tab.

④ Click the Auto-hide the taskbar check box (☐ changes to ☑).

⑤ Click OK.

● Windows Vista hides all but a small strip of the taskbar.

⑥ To view and work with the taskbar, move the mouse pointer to the bottom of the screen.

TIPS

More Options!

If you do not want to see the taskbar at all, follow steps **1** to **3**, click to uncheck the Keep the taskbar on top of other windows check box (☑ changes to ☐) and then click OK. Note that after you do this, the only way to display the taskbar is to press the Windows Logo key or Ctrl+Esc.

Did You Know?

If you have a large monitor, you can increase the size of the taskbar to show more buttons. First unlock the taskbar by right-clicking it and, if you see a check mark beside Lock the Taskbar, click that command. Now move the mouse pointer over the top edge of the taskbar and then click and drag the edge up until the taskbar is the size you want.

Run a program in
COMPATIBILITY MODE

If you are having trouble running an older program, you can customize the program's icon to run in compatibility mode so that it will work properly under Windows Vista.

For best performance and stability, you should try wherever possible to only run programs that were designed for Windows Vista. This is not always practical, however, so it is likely that you have some older programs that came about prior to Windows Vista. In most cases, those older programs should run without any problems under Windows Vista. However, in some cases these older programs fail to run or experience problems in Windows Vista.

The most common reason for such problems is that the older program was designed specifically to run under a particular operating system. For example, a program might have been designed for Windows 95 or Windows 98, and if the program encounters any other operating system it will either refuse to run or it will display frequent glitches.

You can usually work around such problems by running the program in *compatibility mode*, where Windows Vista sets up an environment that mimics the operating system for which the program was designed.

① Click Start.

② Click All Programs.

③ Open the menu that contains the icon of the program you want to configure.

④ Right-click the icon.

⑤ Click Properties.

The program's Properties dialog box appears.

⑥ Click the Compatibility tab.

17

DIFFICULTY LEVEL

⑦ Click the Run this program in compatibility mode for check box (☐ changes to ☑).

⑧ Click the down arrow and then click the operating system for which the program was designed.

⑨ Click OK.

Windows Vista runs the program in compatibility mode each time you start it.

Note: *If you have an older program that requires elevated privileges, see Task #5.*

TIPS

More Options!

Some older programs do not run under Windows Vista because they require fewer colors than Windows Vista displays. For example, many older programs can use at most 256 colors, but the Windows Vista minimum is 65,536 colors. To fix this, follow steps **1** to **6**, click the Run in 256 colors check box (☐ changes to ☑), and then click OK.

More Options!

Another reason some older programs do not work with Windows Vista is because they expect a screen resolution of 640x480, and the minimum resolution under Vista is 800x600. To solve this problem, follow steps **1** to **6**, click the Run in 640 x 480 screen resolution check box (☐ changes to ☑), and then click OK.

Configure
AUTOPLAY DEFAULT ACTIONS

You can customize Windows Vista to perform a specific action whenever you insert a particular type of media, such as an audio CD.

When you insert some types of media into your computer, you usually see a dialog box that gives you a list of actions you can perform on that media. For example, if you insert an audio CD, you have the choice of playing the CD in Windows Media Player, ripping the songs from the CD to Windows Media Player, playing the CD in Media Center, and so on.

This is called AutoPlay and it works for the following media types: audio CDs, DVD movies, enhanced audio CDs and DVDs, software and games, pictures, video files, audio files, blank CDs and DVDs, HD DVD movies, audio DVDs, video CDs, and Super Video CDs.

If you always select the same action for a particular media type, you can bypass the AutoPlay dialog box and have Windows Vista perform that action automatically.

① Click Start.

② Click Control Panel.

The Control Panel window appears.

③ Click Hardware and Sound.

The Hardware and Sound window appears.

④ Click AutoPlay.

18

DIFFICULTY LEVEL

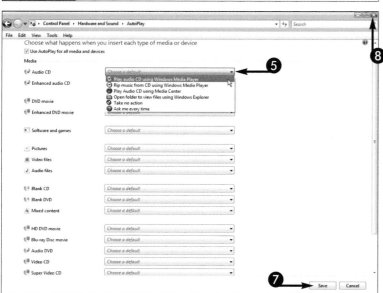

The AutoPlay window appears.

⑤ For the media type you want to configure, click the down arrow and then click the default action that you want Windows Vista to perform when you insert the media.

⑥ Repeat step **5** for the other media you want to configure.

⑦ Click Save.

⑧ Click the Close box to close Control Panel.

Windows Vista performs the default actions you chose whenever you insert the configured media.

Reverse It!

If you do not like the default action you have chosen for a media type, follow steps **1** to **4** to display the AutoPlay window. Click the down arrow (⏷) for the media type, and then click Ask me every time. If you prefer to reset all the media, scroll down to the bottom of the AutoPlay window and then click Reset all defaults. Click Save.

Remove It!

If you prefer that Windows Vista not take any action when you insert any type of media, you can turn off the AutoPlay feature. Follow steps **1** to **4** to display the AutoPlay window and then click to uncheck the Use AutoPlay for all media and devices check box (☑ changes to ☐). Click Save.

Change a
DISK'S DRIVE LETTER

You can tell Windows Vista to use a different letter for a disk drive on your system, which often makes it easier to work with your drives.

The disk drives on your computer are each assigned a letter. On most systems, the floppy drive is usually drive A and the main hard drive is usually drive C. Drives D, E, F, and so on are assigned to other hard drives, as well as CD and DVD drives, depending on the system's configuration. Also, if you insert a removable media, such as a Flash drive or a memory card reader, Windows Vista assigns the first available letters to these drives.

There may be times when the letters that Windows Vista assigns are not suitable. For example, suppose you insert a Flash drive and Vista assigns it the letter E, and then you add a second hard drive to your system and Vista assigns it the letter F. If you then remove the Flash drive, you end up with a gap in your drive letters. That does not cause any serious problems, but it might confuse a novice user. Windows Vista enables you to change the letter that is associated with a disk drive.

① Click Start.

② Right-click Computer.

③ Click Manage.

Note: If the User Account Control dialog box appears, click Continue or type an administrator password and click Submit.

The Computer Management window appears.

④ Click Disk Management.

⑤ Right-click the drive with which you want to work.

⑥ Click Change Drive Letter and Paths.

The Change Drive Letters and Paths dialog box appears.

⑦ Click Change.

The Change Drive Letter or Path dialog box appears.

⑧ Click the down arrow and then click the new drive letter.

⑨ Click OK.

Windows Vista asks you to confirm the change.

⑩ Click Yes.

● Windows Vista changes the drive letter.

⑪ Click the Close box to close the Computer Management window.

Windows Vista uses the new letter for the disk drive.

TIPS

Caution!

If you are going to change the drive letter for a hard drive, be sure to make the change before you install any programs on the drive. Otherwise, changing the drive letter will likely cause those programs to stop working and you would need to uninstall and then reinstall the programs.

Try This!

If your system has multiple hard drives with multiple partitions, several CD and DVD drives, and one or more memory card readers, it is possible that you might run out of drive letters. To work around this problem, mount a drive as a folder to free up its drive letter. Follow steps **1** to **7**, click Add, select the (empty) folder, and click OK. Windows Vista mounts the drive contents in the folder.

Scale the screen to
MAKE TEXT MORE READABLE

If you are having trouble reading the text on the screen, you can scale the screen to a higher dots per inch setting to make the text more readable.

Running Windows Vista at a high resolution is useful because it means you can fit more items on the screen at once because everything appears smaller. The downside is that, depending on the resolution, some fonts may be too small to read comfortably.

You can solve this problem by increasing the Windows Vista dots per inch (DPI) setting. The default is 96 DPI, which means that Windows Vista uses 96 pixels (dots) for every inch of screen space.

(Physical measurements are relative to the screen resolution, so a one-inch line may not actually be one inch long on your screen.)

For example, a line that is meant to be one inch long will be drawn using 96 pixels. However, if you increase the DPI setting, the line appears longer. For example, if you change the DPI to 120, then Windows Vista will scale the screen to use 120 pixels to create the same line. In other words, if you scale the DPI setting up, everything on the screen appears larger, including the text, which makes it easier to read.

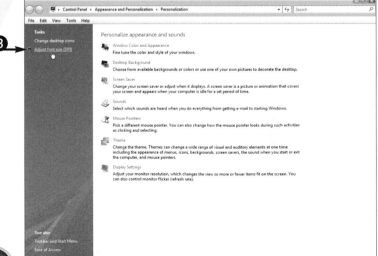

① Right-click the desktop.

② Click Personalize.

The Personalization window appears.

③ Click Adjust font size (DPI).

Note: If the User Account Control dialog box appears, click Continue or type an administrator password and click Submit.

The DPI Scaling dialog box appears.

④ Click Larger scale (120 DPI).

⑤ Click OK.

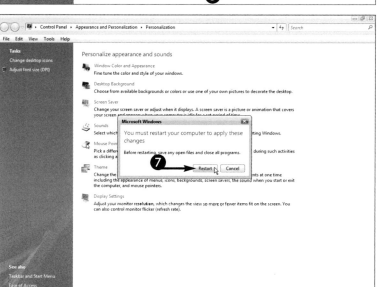

Windows Vista tells you that you must restart your computer for the change to take effect.

⑥ Close any documents and programs you have open.

⑦ Click Restart.

Windows Vista restarts and puts the new font scaling into effect.

More Options!

The DPI Scaling dialog box has two possible values: 96 and 120. However, for some monitors these values to do not provide the best balance between readability and how much information fits on the screen. The solution is to specify a custom DPI value by clicking Custom DPI and typing a percentage value in the text box.

Caution!

It is possible to scale the DPI beyond your screen resolution, which means that parts of the display no longer fit on the screen. This can make it impossible to see the entire Start menu or all the controls in a dialog box. To avoid this, scale back the DPI or increase your screen resolution to compensate.

Control the
NOTIFICATION AREA ICONS

You can customize the way that Windows Vista displays the icons in the notification area to give yourself more room on the taskbar or to ensure a particular icon is always visible.

The notification area on the right side of the taskbar is often a very busy place. Windows Vista itself has at least a couple of dozen icons that it displays, and third-party programs often add their own icons. Unfortunately, having two many icons in the notification area means you have less room for

taskbar buttons, and it also makes the notification area less useful because it becomes hard to keep track of so many icons.

Windows Vista enables you to solve this problem by turning off the display of some system icons, and hiding other icons when they are not in use. Windows Vista also enables you to permanently hide icons that you never use, and to always show icons that you find the most useful.

① Right-click an empty section of the notification area.

② Click Properties.

The Taskbar and Start Menu Properties dialog box appears.

③ Click the Notification Area tab.

④ Click to uncheck the system icon you do not want to appear in the notification area (☑ changes to ☐).

⑤ Click the Hide inactive icons check box (☐ changes to ☑).

⑥ Click Customize.

The Customize Icons dialog box appears.

Note: You can get to the Customize Icons dialog box directly by right-clicking an empty section of the notification area and then clicking Customize Notification Icons.

⑦ Click the icon with which you want to work.

⑧ Click here and then click Hide when inactive (hides the icon when it is not in use), Hide (never displays the icon), or Show (always displays the icon).

⑨ Click OK.

⑩ Click OK.

Windows Vista puts the new settings into effect.

● Click this arrow to see your hidden icons.

TIPS

Did You Know?

One of the most annoying notification area prompts is when the Windows Security Alerts icon warns you that "Your computer might be at risk" because it could not detect an antivirus program. If you have an antivirus program on your computer, you can ignore this prompt, or use the technique in the next tip to turn it off.

Desktop Trick!

To stop this prompt, first double-click the Windows Security Alerts icon to open the Windows Security Center. In the Malware protection area, click Show me my available options. In the Choose an antivirus option dialog box, click "I have an antivirus program that I'll monitor myself" option. If you see the User Account Control dialog box, click Continue or type an administrator password and click Submit

Enrich Your Media Experience

Windows Vista was designed from the ground up to offer you a rich media experience. Whether you are dealing with drawings, photos, sounds, audio CDs, downloaded music files, or DVDs, the tools that are built-in to Windows Vista enable you to play, edit, and even create media.

The downside to having a rich media environment at your fingertips is that the media tools themselves are necessarily feature-laden and complex. The basic operations are usually easy enough to master, but some of the more useful and interesting features tend to be in hard-to-find places. This chapter helps you take advantage of many of these off-the-beaten-track features by showing you how to find and use them.

For example, you discover lots of useful image tips and tricks, including how to rotate an image, repair image defects such as incorrect exposure and red eye, add tags to help you categorize and find your images, and create custom file names for imported images. For videos, you find out how to create clips from a video file and how to trim a video.

On the audio front, you figure out how to adjust the settings Windows Media Player uses to rip audio tracks from a CD, how to share you media library with other people on your network, how to set up an automatic playlist, and how to control the value of a specific program.

Top 100

ROTATE
an image

You can ensure that the subject of an image is right-side up by rotating the image clockwise or counterclockwise as needed.

When you take a vertical shot with your digital camera, your photo appears sideways when you download the image to your computer. Windows Vista often detects photos with an incorrect rotation and asks if you want the rotation corrected during the download. If you elected not to have the rotation fixed, you can still repair the rotation yourself.

Rotation problems are also common with scanned images, because often the only way some images will fit on the scanner bed it to place them sideways. Windows Vista does not offer to correct such images during scanning, so you need to repair the rotation yourself.

In both cases, you can use the Windows Photo Gallery to fix any rotation problems you have with an image.

① Click Start.

② Click All Programs.

③ Click Windows Photo Gallery.

Windows Photo Gallery appears.

④ Click the image you want to rotate.

⑤ Click this button to rotate the image counterclockwise.

● If you prefer to rotate the image clockwise, click this button, instead.

You can also rotate the image by right-clicking it and then clicking either Rotate Counterclockwise or Rotate Clockwise.

● Windows Photo Gallery rotates the image.

⑥ Repeat steps **4** and **5** to rotate any other images that require adjusting.

⑦ Click Close box to close Windows Photo Gallery.

TIPS

Did You Know?
If you use the Rotate Counterclockwise and Rotate Clockwise features frequently, you should know there are keyboard shortcuts you can use. Press Ctrl+, to rotate the image counterclockwise; press Ctrl+. to rotate the image clockwise.

More Options!
If you do not want Windows Photo Gallery to rotate images as you import them from your digital camera, you can turn this feature off. Click File and then click Options to display the Windows Photo Gallery Options dialog box. Click the Import tab and then click to uncheck the Rotate pictures on import check box (☑ changes to ☐). Click OK.

REPAIR
a digital photo

You can use the Windows Vista new Photo Gallery to improve the look of digital photos and other images. The Photo Gallery includes a special Fix window that offers a number of tools to repair various image attributes, including the exposure, colors, and red eye.

For the exposure, Photo Gallery can adjust both the brightness of the image and the image contrast, which is the relative difference between the lightest and darkest areas in the image.

For the color, Photo Gallery can adjust the color temperature (the relative warmth of the colors, where cooler means bluer and hotter means redder), the tint, and the saturation (the percentage of hue in each color).

Photo Gallery also enables you crop an image to remove unwanted subjects or to ensure that the main subject is centered in the photo.

Photo Gallery maintains a backup of the original photo, so you can always reverse any adjustments you make.

① Click Start.

② Click All Programs.

③ Click Windows Photo Gallery.

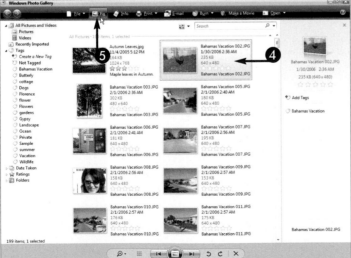

Windows Photo Gallery appears.

④ Click the image you want to repair.

⑤ Click Fix.

The Fix window appears.

6 To change the exposure, click Adjust Exposure and then click and drag the Brightness and Contrast sliders.

7 To change the color, click Adjust Color and then click and drag the Color Temperature, Tint, and Saturation sliders.

● If you are not sure how to use these tools, click Auto Adjust to have Photo Gallery make the adjustments for you.

8 To remove red eye from a photo, click Fix Red Eye.

9 To crop the picture, first click Crop Picture.

10 Click here and then click the dimensions you want.

11 Click and drag the handles to set the new size of the image.

12 Click Apply.

13 When you are done, click Back to Gallery.

Photo Gallery applies the repairs.

TIPS

More Options!

When you crop an image, Photo Gallery assumes you want the cropped version to have the same relative height and width of the original. If you do not want this, click down arrow (⊡) in the Proportion list and then click Custom. If you are cropping for a photo printout, click one of the standard sizes, such as 5" x 7", instead.

Reverse It!

The Photo Gallery always keeps a backup copy of the original image, just in case. To undo all your changes and get the original image back, click the image and then click Fix. In the Fix window, click Revert and then click Revert to Original (or press Ctrl+R). When Windows Photo Gallery asks you to confirm, click Revert.

CATEGORIZE YOUR IMAGES
with tags

By adding special keywords called tags to your images, you can create categories that make it easier to view and work with related images.

If you have images that are related in some way, one way to work with them efficiently is to store them in the same folder. However, this is not always convenient. For example, if you went on recent trips to France, Germany, and Italy, it makes sense to store the photos from those trips in three separate folders. However, if you need to work with all those photos — for example, to create a DVD of your

European photos — then having them in separate folders is inconvenient.

The solution is to use the Windows Photo Gallery tag feature. A *tag* is a keyword (or possibly a key phrase) that describes an image. In the previous example, you could apply the keyword Europe to all of the photos from France, Germany, and Italy.

Windows Photo Gallery comes with a few tags, including Dogs, Flowers, and Sunsets, but you can create as many as you need.

APPLY TAGS TO IMAGES

① Click Start.

② Click All Programs.

③ Click Windows Photo Gallery.

Windows Photo Gallery appears.

④ Click Info.

The Info pane appears.

⑤ Click the image with which you want to work.

⑥ Click Add Tags.

- A text box appears.

7 Type a tag and press Enter.

- Tags you have added appear here.

8 Repeat steps **5** and **6** to add more tags to the image.

9 Repeat steps **4** to **7** to add tags to other images.

10 Click the Hide Info Pane button.

The Info pane disappears.

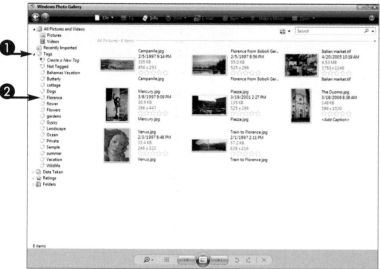

USE A TAG TO FILTER IMAGES

1 Click Tags.

2 Click the tag.

Windows Photo Gallery displays only the images that have the selected tag applied.

TIPS

More Options!

If you create a tag that you do not like or that is not descriptive enough, you can rename it to something better. Click Tags to display the list of tags, right-click the tag you want to change, and then click Rename. Type the new tag text and press Enter.

Reverse It!

If you accidentally apply the wrong tag to an image, you should remove the tag to avoid cluttering your folders with erroneous images. Click Info to display the Info pane and then click the image. Right-click the incorrect tag and then click Remove Tag.

CREATE CUSTOM NAMES
for imported images

You can create more meaningful file names for your imported images by configuring Windows Photo Gallery to use a custom name that you specify during each import operation.

When you import images from a device such as a digital camera, Windows Photo Gallery launches the Windows Picture and Video Import tool to handle the job. By default, this tool preserves the existing file names of the images. However, most devices supply images with cryptic file names, such as IMG_1083 and scan001. These non-descriptive names can make it more difficult to find and work with images,

particularly if you use the Details view in the Pictures folder.

To work around this problem, you can configure the Windows Picture and Video Import tool to apply a custom name to your imported images. This custom name is based on an *event tag* — a word or short phrase — that you specify during the import operation. For example, if you specify Bahamas Vacation as the event tag, then your imported images will be named Bahamas Vacation 001, Bahamas Vacation 002, and so on.

❶ Click Start.

❷ Click All Programs.

❸ Click Windows Photo Gallery.

Windows Photo Gallery appears.

❹ Click File.

❺ Click Options.

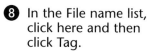

The Windows Photo Gallery Options dialog box appears.

⑥ Click the Import tab.

⑦ In the Settings for list, click here and then click the type of device with which you want to work.

⑧ In the File name list, click here and then click Tag.

⑨ Repeat steps **7** and **8** to apply the event tag file name to imports from other devices.

##25

⑩ Click the Prompt for a tag on import check box (☐ changes to ☑).

⑪ Click OK.

Windows Photo Gallery puts the new settings into effect.

TIPS

Did You Know?

You can configure Windows Vista to always launch the Windows Picture and Video Import tool when you connect your digital camera. In the Import tab, click the Change default autoplay options option to display the AutoPlay window. In the Pictures list, click the down arrow (▾) and then click Import pictures using Windows. Click Save.

More Options!

If you always clear the memory card in your digital camera after you import the images, you can have the Windows Picture and Video Import tool do this for you automatically. In the Import tab, click the Always erase from camera after importing check box (☐ changes to ☑).

SYNCHRONIZE
a media device

If you have a portable media device that is compatible with Windows Media Player, you synchronize that device with Media Player to ensure the device always has the music you want.

Windows Media Player supports a wide range of portable media devices. These devices include MP3 players, memory cards, Smartphones, digital audio receivers, wired and wireless network media players, and portable media centers.

When you insert a Media Player-compatible device, Media Player recognizes the device and automatically displays the device, its total capacity, and its available space in the Media Player Sync tab.

You can then specify a sync list of music files on your computer. Media Player can add those files to the device, and then keep your computer and the device synchronized as the sync list changes.

The Windows Vista version of Media Player supports two-way syncing, which means that not only can you sync files from your PC to a media device, but you also can sync files from a media device to your PC.

① Attach the media device to your computer.

② Click Start.

③ Click All Programs.

④ Click Windows Media Player.

Windows Media Player appears.

⑤ Click the Sync tab.

- Information about the device appears here.

6 Click and drag music from your library and drop it inside the Sync List.

- Media Player updates the space remaining on the device.

7 Click Start Sync.

Media Player adds the music to the device.

TIPS

Important!

If the music you added to the device comes from a variety of genres, albums, or artists, save the sync list as a playlist so you do not have to re-create the sync list in the future. After you have built the sync list, pull down the Sync List menu, click Save Playlist As, type a name for the playlist, and click Save. The next time you want to sync the device, click and drag the playlist into the Sync List.

Check It Out!

If you are not sure whether a device you have is compatible with Media Player, or if you are thinking of purchasing a media device and want to ensure it is Media Player-compatible, look for the Plays for Sure logo on the box. If you are still not sure, you can search for the device at the Plays for Sure Web site at www.playsforsure.com.

Create an
AUTOMATIC PLAYLIST

You can create a playlist that Media Player maintains automatically based on the criteria you specify.

You normally create a playlist by clicking and dragging music files to the playlist. However, you can also create a playlist based on the properties that Media Player maintains for each file. These properties include Album Artist, Genre, Composer, and Rating, to name just a few. So, for example, you could create a playlist that includes every music file where the Genre property equals Classical.

You create a property-based playlist by specifying the playlist *criteria*, which consists of three factors: the property, the property value, and an operator that relates the two. The most common operators are Is, Is Not, and Contains. For the classical music example, the criteria would be the following: Genre Is Classical.

The best part about property-based playlists is that they are automatic. This means that after you set up the playlist, Media Player automatically populates the playlist with all the music files that meet your criteria.

① In Windows Media Player, click the arrow below the Library tab.

② Click Create Auto Playlist.

The New Auto Playlist dialog box appears.

③ Type a name for the playlist.

④ Click here to display the menu of properties.

⑤ Click a property.

6 Click here to choose an operator.

7 Click here and then click the criteria you want to use.

8 Click OK.

DIFFICULTY LEVEL

● Media Player adds your playlist to My Playlists.

● Media Player populates the playlist based on your criteria.

TIPS

More Options!

You can place restrictions on your automatic playlists so that they do not become too large. Open the Playlists branch, right-click your automatic playlist, and then click Edit to display the Edit Auto Playlist dialog box. Pull down the list named and apply the following restrictions to the auto playlist, and then click Limit Number of Items, Limit Total Duration To, or Limit Total Size To. Fill in the limit, and then click OK.

Remove It!

If you no longer need your automatic playlist, you should delete it so that Media Player does not keep updating it and to reduce clutter in the Playlists branch. Right-click the playlist and then click Delete. In the confirmation dialog box that appears, click Delete from library and my computer, and then click OK.

Adjust
RIP SETTINGS

Windows Media Player gives you lots of control over the copying — or *ripping* — of tracks from an audio CD by enabling you to select a format and a bit rate.

The *format* is the audio file type you want to use to store the ripped tracks on your computer. You have six choices:

The Windows Media Audio format compresses audio by removing extraneous sounds that are not normally detected by the human ear.

The Windows Media Audio (variable bit rate) format changes the compression depending on the audio data: if the data is more complex, it uses less compression to keep the quality high.

The Windows Media Audio Lossless format does not compress the audio tracks.

The MP3 format also compresses the audio files to make them smaller, but MP3s are generally about twice the size of WMA files.

The WAV format is an uncompressed audio file format that is compatible with all versions of Windows.

The *bit rate* determines the quality of the rip and is measured in kilobits per second (Kbps). The higher the bit rate, the better the quality, but the more hard drive space each track uses.

① In Windows Media Player, click the arrow below the Rip tab.

② Click Format.

Windows Media Player displays the available audio file formats.

③ Click the format you want to use.

DIFFICULTY LEVEL

④ Click the arrow below the Rip tab.

⑤ Click Bit Rate.

Windows Media Player displays the available bit rates.

*Note: The available bit rates depend on the audio file format you chose in step **3**. Note that some formats use a fixed bit rate that you cannot change.*

⑥ Click the bit rate you want to use.

Windows Media Player uses the selected format and bit rate the next time you rip tracks from an audio CD.

TIP

Did You Know?

The bit rate determines the size of each ripped track. There are 8 bits in a byte, 1,024 bytes in a kilobyte, and 1,024 kilobytes in a megabyte. The following table lists the bit rates for the Windows Media Audio format and how much drive space it uses:

Bit Rates and Drive Space for the WMA Format		
Bit Rate (Kbps)	**KB/Minute**	**MB/Hour**
48	360	21
64	480	28
96	720	42
128	960	56
160	1,200	70
192	1,440	84

CUSTOMIZE
the Media Player view

You can see just the information you want for every media file by customizing the Media Player view to show the specific media details you prefer.

Windows Media Player keeps track of a great deal of information for all your media files. For music files, Media Player keeps tracks of standard properties, such as the album title, artist, and the track names and lengths. However, Media Player also stores more detailed information, such as the genre, release date, bit rate, file format, and size.

For videos, Media Player stores standard properties, such as the title, length, and size, but also in some cases more detailed information, such as number of frames per second and the bit rate for both the video and audio tracks. For some commercial videos, you can also view the director, actors, and studio.

These properties are called *metadata*, because they are all data that describe the media. You can customize any of the Media Player folders to display the Details view, which shows the metadata. Further, you can customize the specific metadata columns that Media Player displays in each view.

SWITCH TO DETAILS VIEW

❶ Click here to open the View Options menu.

❷ Click Details.

Media Player switches to Details view.

CUSTOMIZE COLUMNS

❸ Click here to open the Layout Options menu.

❹ Click Choose Columns.

The Choose Columns dialog box appears.

5 Click the deactivated check boxes of the columns you want to view (☐ changes to ☑).

6 Click to uncheck the activated check boxes of the columns you do not want to view (☑ changes to ☐).

DIFFICULTY LEVEL

7 To move the selected column to the left in Details view, click Move Up.

8 To move the selected column to the right in Details view, click Move Down.

9 Click OK.

● Media Player updates the view to display the columns you selected.

More Options!
You can see more columns in Details view if you reduce the width of each column so that it is just wide enough to display its data. The easiest way to do this is to move the mouse pointer over the right edge of the column's header — the pointer changes to a two-headed arrow with vertical bar through it — and then double-click.

More Options!
You can change the order of the Details view columns without displaying the Choose Columns dialog box. Instead, use your mouse to click and drag the column header to the left or right and then drop it in the new position.

SHARE YOUR MEDIA LIBRARY
with others

You can listen to the songs and view the photos and videos in your Media Player Library on another device by sharing your Library over a wired or wireless network.

If you have spent a great deal of time ripping audio CDs, downloading music files, adding other media to your Library, and organizing the Library, you probably do not want to repeat all that work on another computer. If you have a wired or wireless network, however, you can take advantage of the Library work

you have done on one computer by sharing that Library over the network. This enables any other computer using Windows Vista to include your media in that machine's Media Player Library. This also applies to other user accounts on your computer. Those users can log on and then access your shared Library.

Your shared Library is also available to other media devices on the network, such as an Xbox 360 or a networked digital media receiver.

➊ In Windows Media Player, click the arrow below the Library tab.

➋ Click Media Sharing.

The Media Sharing dialog box appears.

➌ Click the Share my media to check box (☐ changes to ☑).

Media Player displays icons for each device that you can share your media with.

● Approved for sharing.

● Denied sharing.

● Not yet configured.

④ Click the device you want to work with.

⑤ Click Allow.

● If you do not want to share your media with a device, click Deny, instead.

Note: *If the User Account Control dialog box appears, click Continue or type an administrator password and click Submit.*

⑥ Click OK.

Media Player shares your media on the network.

TIPS

More Options!

If you want to restrict the media that you share, open the Media Sharing dialog box and click Settings to open the Default Settings dialog box. In the Media types group, click the check boxes of the media types you do not want to share (☑ changes to ☐). You can also restrict the media based on the ratings and on parental rating. Click OK to put the settings into effect.

Apply It!

When you allow sharing with another device, the media that the other device is sharing is added to the Media Player Navigation pane. To use the shared media from another device, open the device's branch in the Navigation pane and then select a folder: Artist, Songs, Playlists, and so on.

Display the Windows Media Player
TOOLBAR

You can control the playback of Windows Media Player, without leaving your current program, by activating and using the program's taskbar toolbar.

Many people like to use Windows Media Player as a background program while they do work in another program. For example, they may listen to an audio CD or downloaded music while using a word processor or reading and composing e-mail messages.

This works well except when you want to make playback adjustments, such as skipping a track,

changing the volume, or pausing the media while you take a phone call. You must switch from your current program to Windows Media Player, make the adjustments, and then return to your work.

Instead of switching from your current program to Windows Media Player and then back again, you can display the program's taskbar toolbar — a feature called *mini-mode*. This toolbar appears on the Windows Vista taskbar and enables you to pause playback, skip tracks, and mute or change the volume.

① Click the Minimize button.

Windows Vista asks if you want the Windows Media Player toolbar on your taskbar.

② Click Yes.

The Windows Media Player toolbar appears in place of the Windows Media Player taskbar button.

Note: The Windows Media Player toolbar now appears each time you minimize the program. You do not need to repeat this step in the future.

DIFFICULTY LEVEL

③ Click Play to begin playback of the currently selected media.

● You can click the Volume button to adjust the playback volume.

● You can click Show Video and Visualization window button to show or hide the Video and Visualization window.

Note: The Video and Visualization window shows the current visualization (if music is playing) or the current video. The window appears on top of any other window on your screen.

④ Click the Restore button to restore the Windows Media Player window.

The Windows Media Player reappears.

TIPS

Did You Know?
The Mini Player toolbar's Restore button (▣) is a tiny target that is difficult to click with the mouse. To bypass the mouse and restore Windows Media Player via the keyboard, press Alt+Shift+P.

Reverse It!
If you do not want the Windows Media Player toolbar to appear in the taskbar when you minimize the program, you can turn it off. Right-click an empty section of the taskbar, click Toolbars, and then click Windows Media Player.

Get the Most Out of
Your Files and Folders

Although you may use Windows Vista to achieve certain ends — writing memos and letters, create presentations, play games, surf the Internet, and so on — you still have to deal with files and folders as part of your day-to-day work or play. Basic tasks such as copying and moving files, creating and renaming folders, and deleting unneeded files and folders are part of the Windows Vista routine.

Your goal should be to make all this humdrum folder maintenance lesson a nuisance, so you have more time doing the more interesting and to more worthy pursuits. Fortunately, Windows Vista offers a number of shortcuts and techniques that can shorten file and folder tasks and make them more efficient. In this chapter you learn a number of these techniques.

For example, you learn how to open folders and launch files with just a single-click of the mouse instead of the usual double-click. You learn how to open a file in a program other than the one with which it is associated. You learn how to customize the Send To menu to make moving files even faster. You also learn how to perform an advanced search; how to compress and stack files to make them easier to find and manage; how to revert to a previous version of a file; and how to synchronize files with another PC.

Top 100

Open your files and folders with a
SINGLE-CLICK

You can open files and folders more quickly and consistently by customizing Windows Vista to open items with a single mouse click instead of a double-click.

Double-clicking is not a difficult skill to learn, but it can be hard to master. For example, if you wait too long between clicks or if you move the mouse pointer slightly between the first and second click, Windows Vista interprets your action as two single-clicks instead of a double-click.

This can really slow you down. In a folder, for example, clicking a file twice opens the file name text box for editing. This means you first have to click elsewhere in the folder or press Esc to close the text box, and then you have to try your double-click again.

For all these reasons, opening files and folders with a single-click is not only faster but also more efficient. This has the added advantage of making Windows Vista more consistent; for example, you already open items on the Start menu with a single-click.

① In any folder window, click the Organize list's menu.

② Click Folder and Search Options.

The Folder Options dialog box appears.

③ Click the General tab.

④ Click the Single-click to open an item (point to select) option (○ changes to ◉).

⑤ Click OK.

● When you hover the mouse pointer over a file or folder, Windows Vista places an underline under the icon label to remind you to use a single-click.

Note: With single-clicking activated, you select a file or folder by pointing at it with your mouse pointer.

TIPS

More Options!
To make it easier to remember to single-click, you can configure Windows Vista to underline *all* your files and folders. Follow steps **1** to **4** in this task and then click the Underline icon titles consistent with my browser option (○ changes to ◉). Click OK to put the new setting into effect. If you think the underlines make your folders look cluttered, follow steps **1** to **4** and click the Underline icon titles only when I point at them option (○ changes to ◉).

Reverse It!
If you do not like single-clicking or you cannot get used to it, you can return to double-clicking. Follow steps **1** to **4** in this task and then click the Double-click to open an item option (○ changes to ◉). Click OK to put the new setting into effect.

Open a file with a
DIFFERENT PROGRAM

You can open a file in a different program from the one that is normally associated with the file. This enables you to use the other program's features to work on the file.

Every document you create has a particular file type. File types are Text Documents, Rich Text Documents, Bitmap Images, JPEG Images, and more. All these types have a default program associated with them. For example, Text Documents are associated with

Notepad, and Rich Text Documents are associated with WordPad or Word. Double-clicking a file opens the file in the associated program.

You may have situations where you prefer to open a particular file with a different program. For example, double-clicking a picture file opens it in the Photo Gallery Viewer. However, you may prefer to open the picture file in Paint or some other image editing program so that you can make changes to the picture.

① Open the folder that contains the file you want to open.

② Click the file.

③ Click the Preview menu.

● If the program you want to use appears here, click the program and skip the remaining steps.

④ Click Choose Default Program.

The Open With dialog box appears.

⑤ If you do not see a list of programs, double-click Other Programs.

⑥ Click the program you want to use to open the file.

● If the program you want to use does not appear in the list, you can click Browse and use the new Open With dialog box to specify the program.

⑦ Click to uncheck the Always use the selected program to open this kind of file check box (☑ changes to ☐).

⑧ Click OK.

Windows Vista opens the file in the program you chose.

TIPS

More Options!
Besides opening the file you selected in the new program, you may prefer to open every other file of the same type — such as Text documents or Rich Text Format documents — in the same program. Follow steps **1** to **5** and then click the Always use the selected program to open this kind of file check box (☐ changes to ☑).

Did You Know?
Windows Vista enables you to set the default program for a number of file types at once. Click Start, click Default Programs, and then click Associate a file type or protocol with a program. For each file type, click the file type, click Change program, and then follow steps **5** and **7**.

Add destinations to your
SEND TO MENU

You can enhance the value of the Send To menu, making copying files and folders faster, by customizing the menu with your own destinations.

After you right-click a file or folder, you can then click Send To to reveal the Windows Vista Send To menu. This handy menu offers a number of destinations, depending on your computer's configuration: Compressed (zipped) Folder, Desktop (create shortcut), Documents, Fax Recipient, and Mail Recipient. You may also see other removable disk drives, such as a recordable CD drive. When you click one of these destinations, Windows Vista sends a

copy of the selected file or folder to that location. This is much faster than copying the item, finding and opening the destination folder, and then pasting the item.

So making a good thing even better by adding your own destinations to the Send To menu is a great idea. You can add a favorite folder, a folder that you use for backup copies, a folder for a current project, a disk drive, the Recycle Bin, or a network folder. You can even add a printer for quick printing to a specific device.

❶ Press Windows Logo+R.

The Run dialog box appears.

❷ Type **%userprofile%\ appdata\Roaming\ Microsoft\Windows\ SendTo**.

❸ Click OK.

The SendTo window appears.

● The window shows all the items in the Send To menu, except for your floppy and removable drives.

4 Open the folder containing the destination you want to add to the Send To menu.

This example uses Conference Files as the destination folder.

5 Right-click and drag the destination item and drop it in the SendTo window.

6 Click Create Shortcuts Here from the menu that appears after you drop the item.

● Windows Vista adds a shortcut for the destination in the SendTo window.

● The destination now appears in the Send To menu. To view it, you can click any file or folder, File, and then Send To.

TIPS

Customize It!

You can customize the Send To menu with more than just folders. For example, if your system has multiple printers, you can add them to the Send To menu and then easily send a document to any printer. To add a printer to the Send To menu, click Start and then Control Panel. In the Control Panel window, click Printers. Click and drag the printer to drop it in the SendTo window.

Customize It!

You can also add a program to the Send To menu. When you send a document to the program, the document opens in that program automatically. To add a program to the Send To menu, click Start, click All Programs, and open the menu that contains an icon for the program. Click and drag the program icon to drop it in the SendTo window

Chapter 4: Get the Most Out of Your Files and Folders 77

Protect a file by making it
READ-ONLY

You can prevent other people from making changes to an important file by designating the file as read-only.

Much day-to-day work in Windows Vista is required but not terribly important. Most memos, letters, and notes are run-of-the-mill and do not require extra security. Occasionally, however, you may create or work with a file that *is* important. It could be a carefully crafted letter, a memo detailing important company strategy, or a collection of hard-won brainstorming notes. Whatever the content, such a file requires extra protection to ensure that you do not lose your work.

You can set advanced file permissions that can prevent a document from being changed or even deleted (see Task #72). If your only concern is preventing other people from making changes to a document, a simpler technique you can use is making the document *read-only*. This means that although other people can make changes to a document, they cannot *save* those changes (except to a new file). This task shows you how to make a file read-only.

MAKE A FILE READ-ONLY

① Open the folder that contains the file with which you want to work.

② Right-click the file.

③ Click Properties.

The file's Properties dialog box appears.

④ Click the General tab.

⑤ Click the Read-only check box (☐ changes to ☑).

⑥ Click OK.

The file is now read-only.

#

1 Double-click a read-only file to open it.

2 Make changes to the file.

3 Click the Save button.

The Save As dialog box appears.

DIFFICULTY LEVEL

4 Click Save.

5 Click Yes.

The program tells you it cannot create (save) the file, confirming that the file is read-only.

6 Click OK.

More Options!

You can hide a file that contains sensitive data to prevent other people from viewing. Follow steps **1** to **4**. Click the Hidden check box (☐ changes to ☑), click OK, and then press F5. The file icon disappears.

Reverse It!

When you want to make changes to the file yourself, you can remove the read-only attribute. Follow steps **1** to **4**, click the Read-only check box (☑ changes to ☐), and then OK.

More Options!

To see a hidden file, open the folder containing the file, click Start, click Control Panel, click Appearance and Personalization, and then click Folder Options. In the Folder Options dialog box, click the View tab, the Show hidden files and folders option (◯ changes to ◉), and then OK.

Perform an
ADVANCED FILE SEARCH

You can take advantage of the many new file properties supported by Windows Vista to search for files based on the author, keywords, and other data.

In Windows Vista, however, you can perform sophisticated searches by using a number of different properties, including some of the new file properties supported by Vista. These file properties are called *metadata*, because they are data that describes the data on your system — that is, your documents.

For example, the Authors property specifies the name of the person (or people) that created a

document. Similarly, the Tags property lists one or more words or phrases that describe the contents of a document. You can create advanced searches that look in these and other properties for the file or files you seek.

Windows Vista also supports advanced searches for particular types of files, including e-mail messages, documents, pictures, and music. For music files, you can search on the Title, Artists, and Album properties. For e-mail, you can search on the Subject, From names, and To names.

PERFORM AN ADVANCED SEARCH USING PROPERTIES

1 Open the folder in which you want to search.

*Note: If you want to search all your documents, click Start, click Search, and then skip to step **5**.*

2 Click the Organize menu.

3 Click Layout.

4 Click Search Pane.

● The Search Pane appears.

5 To search for a particular type of file, click a Show only button.

6 Click Advanced Search.

The Advanced Search options appear.

The fields you see in this screen depend on the type of document you selected in step **5**.

7 Fill in the property values of the documents you want to find.

8 Click Search.

#36

DIFFICULTY LEVEL

● Windows Vista displays the files that match your search criteria.

TIPS

More Options!

When you type a value in a property text box, Windows Vista matches those files where the value is a partial match. For example, if you type allegro in the Title property, Windows Vista matches every music file that contains the word allegro. If you prefer exact matches, click Organize and then Folder and Search Options. Click the Search tab and then click to deactivate the Find partial matches check box (☑ changes to ☐). Click OK.

More Options!

By default, Windows Vista searches inside the current folder and its subfolders. If you want to add another folder to the search, click the Location menu and click Choose search locations. Click the check box beside the folder you want to add (☐ changes to ☑) and then click OK.

Perform an
ADVANCED FILE SEARCH

You can also search for documents based on the date they were created or last modified, as well as the document size.

Searching by date is useful if you know when you created it or last worked with it. Windows Vista enables you to search using three different date types: Date modified, which is the date you last changed the file; Date created, which is the date you originally created the file; and Date accessed, which is the last time you opened the file. In each case, you can also choose one of three date operators:

Is, which matches a specific date; Is before, which matches all dates before the one you specify; and Is after, which matches all dates after the one you specify.

You can also search for documents based on their size. One situation where this comes in handy is when you want to free up disk space by archiving or deleting very large files that you no longer use. To search by size, you first select one of three operators: Equals, Is less than, or Is greater than. You then specify a size, in kilobytes.

PERFORM AN ADVANCED SEARCH BY DATE

1. Follow steps **1** to **6** on the previous pages to display the Advanced Search options.

2. Use this list to click the type of date you want to search.

3. Click here to select the date operator you want to use.

4. Click here to select the calendar date you want to use.

5. Click Search.

   Windows Vista displays the files that match your search criteria.

① Follow steps **1** to **6** on the previous pages to display the Advanced Search options.

② Click here to select the size operator you want to use.

36
CONTINUED

③ Type a size in kilobytes.

④ Click Search.

Windows Vista displays the files that match your search criteria.

Note: See Task #6 to learn how to improve search performance by adding folders to the Windows Vista search index.

Note: See Task #37 to learn how to save your search details and reuse them later on.

TIPS

Did You Know?
After you run the search, you can perform another search quickly by choosing a different operator. Pull down the list of operators, click the operator you want, and then click Search. Windows Vista runs the new search.

Change It!
After you run the search, if you do not see the property you used for the criteria, right-click a column heading, and then click More. In the Choose Details dialog box, click the check box beside the property, and then click OK.

Remove It!
If you have added a date criteria or a size criteria and you decide not to use it, you can remove it. Use the appropriate operator list to select the value.

Save time by
SAVING AND REUSING A SEARCH

If you have a search that you want to run again in the future, you can save the details of the search. This saves you time because instead of defining the same search from scratch, you can simply reuse the saved version.

You can set up and run an advanced search using the Windows Vista search engine (see Task #36). This is a powerful tool for finding files on your system, but setting up a search — particularly one that uses multiple search filters — can be time-consuming.

If there are searches that you plan on running regularly, it is inefficient to have to set up the same search criteria over and over.

The solution to this problem is to save your search as one of the Windows Vista new search folders. A *search folder* is a collection of files and folders from your system that match a specified set of search criteria. After you set up and run a search, you can save it as a search folder and then reuse it anytime you need it.

SAVE A SEARCH

1 Set up and run an advanced search.

   Note: See Task #36 to learn how to create an advanced search.

2 Click Save Search.

The Save As dialog box appears.

3 Type a file name for the search folder.

4 Type one or more tags (this is optional).

5 Click Save.

   Windows Vista saves the search as a search folder.

REUSE A SEARCH

1 In any folder window, click Searches.

The Saved Searches folder appears.

● This folder displays the search folders saved on your system.

2 Double-click the search folder you want to open.

Windows Vista runs the search and displays the results.

TIPS

Did You Know?

Windows Vista comes with six predefined search folders including five that show you recent activity on your computer: Recent Documents, Recent E-mail, Recent Music, Recent Pictures and Videos, and Recently Changed. There is also a Shared By Me search that shows the folders and files you are sharing with other users.

Remove It!

If you no longer need a saved search, you should delete the search folder to reduce the clutter in the Searches folder. Open the Searches folder, click the search folder you want to remove, and then press Delete. When Windows Vista asks you to confirm, click Yes.

Find files faster by
SORTING AND FILTERING

You can find the files in a folder faster by sorting the files based on the values in a property, or by filtering the folder to show only files that have a certain property value.

You can use file metadata (see Task #36) to organize a folder in a way that makes it easier to find the file or files with which you want to work. One way to organize a folder is to sort the files based on the values in a particular file property. By default, most folders display files sorted by the values in the Name (file name) property. However, you can sort files

using the values in any property, including Date Modified, Authors, and Type.

Another way to organize a folder is to *filter* the files based on the unique values in a particular file property. This means that you configure the folder to display only those files that have a particular value in that property. For example, if you use the Type property, you could filter the folder to show only those files where Type is Text Document or MP3 Format Sound.

SORTING FILES

① Open the folder you want to sort.

② Click the column menu you want to use for the sort.

③ Click Sort.

④ Repeat steps **2** and **3** to switch the sort order between ascending and a descending.

Windows Vista sorts the files based on the field.

● This arrow tells you which column is being used to sort the files and it tells you the direction of the sort (up for ascending; down for descending).

#38

DIFFICULTY LEVEL

① Open the folder you want to filter.

② Click a column's menu to display a list of the unique values in the column.

Note: For some columns, Windows Vista displays a range of values instead of specific values. For date-related columns, you also see a calendar that enables you to filter based on a specific date.

③ Click the check box for each value you want to include (☐ changes to ☑).

● Windows Vista filters the files to show just those that have the property value that matches one of the activated check boxes.

● A check mark appears here to indicate that you have applied a filter to the column.

TIPS

Try This!
A quick way to sort the files in a folder is to click the header of the column on which you want to sort the files. Click the header again to switch the sort order.

Customize It!
If you want to sort or filter the folder using a field that is not displayed, right-click any column header and then click the name of the column you want to use. Click More to see a full list of the available columns.

Customize It!
You can also change the order in which the columns appear in the folder window. The easiest way to do this is to move the mouse pointer over a column header, click and drag the mouse, and then drop the column header in the position you want.

Organize files by
GROUPING AND STACKING

You can make the files in a folder easier to manage and work with by organizing them into groups and stacks.

If you have a folder with a large collection of files, managing or working with all those files can be difficult or time-consuming. Windows Vista offers two new file management tools that can help: grouping and stacking.

Grouping files means organizing them into distinct categories based on the property values in a particular column. For example, if you group a folder

based on the Type column, Windows Vista displays files of the same type together in a group. You can then work with that group as a whole — move it, delete it, and so on.

Stacking files also means organizing them based on the unique property values in a particular column. However, each stack is a kind of virtual folder that holds the files that share a particular property value. For example, if you stack a folder based on the Type column, Windows Vista creates virtual folders — *stacks* — for each unique Type value.

GROUP FILES

❶ Open the folder you want to group.

❷ Click the field's menu you want to use for the grouping.

❸ Click Group.

Windows Vista groups the files.

● Each group has its own header that identifies the group and tells you how many files are in the group.

① Open the folder you want to group.

② Click the field's menu you want to use for the stacks.

③ Click Stack by *Field*, where *Field* is the name of the field you are using (for example, Stack by Type).

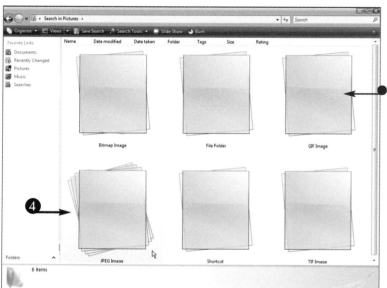

Windows Vista stacks the files.

● Each icon represents a stack.

④ Double-click a stack to open it and see its files.

TIPS

Did You Know?
When you group a folder, you can *collapse* the group — hide everything but the group header — by double-clicking the group header. To *expand* the group — display the group's files — double-click the header again.

Did You Know?
You can also collapse every group by right-clicking any group header and then clicking Collapse all groups. To expand all the groups, right-click any group header and click Expand all groups.

Try This!
In a grouped folder, you can also use the group headers to perform various operations. For example, you can click a group header to select all the files in that group. You can also click and drag the group header to move or copy the entire group to another location.

Move your
DOCUMENTS FOLDER

You can move your Documents folder to another location on your system. This is useful if you want to store your documents on a hard drive with more free space, or if you want to combine Documents with other data files for easier backups.

By default, your Documents folder is located in C:\Users*User*\Documents, where *User* is your Windows Vista user name (the name that appears at the top of the Start menu). However, when you use Documents in your everyday work, this location is transparent to you because Windows Vista enables you to open the folder directly.

That feature is convenient, but what if the default location of the Documents folder becomes a problem? For example, you may find that drive C is running low on hard drive space. Also, many people add to their computer a second hard drive — usually drive D — in which to store their documents. However, having some files in Documents and others in drive D can be a hassle.

To solve both problems, you can move Documents to another location.

① If the folder to which you want to move Documents does not yet exist, create the folder.

② Click Start.

③ Right-click Documents.

④ Click Properties.

The Documents Properties dialog box appears.

⑤ Click the Location tab.

⑥ Click Move.

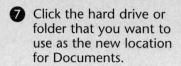

The Select a Destination dialog box appears.

⑦ Click the hard drive or folder that you want to use as the new location for Documents.

⑧ Click Select Folder to return to the Documents Properties dialog box.

● The new location appears in the text box.

⑨ Click OK.

Windows Vista asks you if you want to move the existing Documents folder files to the new location.

⑩ Click Yes.

Windows Vista moves the Documents folder and its files to the new location.

TIPS

Reverse It!

If you decide that you prefer Documents in its original location, you do not need to follow all of the steps in this task to select the original folder. Instead, follow steps **1** to **4** to display the Location tab, click Restore Default, and then click OK.

Apply It!

You can use the technique in this task to move any of your user folders, including Pictures, Music, Videos, Contacts, Downloads, and Favorites. Click Start then click your user name to view all your user folders, right-click the folder you want to move, and then click Properties.

Restore a
PREVIOUS VERSION OF A FILE

If you improperly edit, accidentally delete, or corrupt a file through a system crash, in many cases you can restore a previous version of the file.

Each time you start your computer, Windows Vista takes a "snapshot" of its current contents. As you work on your files throughout the day, Windows Vista keeps track of the changes you make to each file. This gives Windows Vista the capability to reverse the changes you have made to a file to revert to the version of the file that existed when Vista took its system snapshot. An earlier state of a file is called a *previous version*.

Why would you want to revert to a previous version of a file? One reason is that you might improperly edit the file by deleting or changing important data. In some cases you may be able to restore that data by going back to a previous version of the file. Another reason is that the file might become corrupted if the program or Windows Vista crashes. You can get a working version of the file back by restoring to a previous version.

1 Open the folder that contains the file you want to restore.

2 Right-click the file.

3 Click Restore previous versions.

Windows Vista displays the file's Properties dialog box and the Previous Versions tab.

The File versions list shows you the previous versions of the file that exist.

4 Click a previous version.

5 Click Restore.

Windows Vista asks you to confirm that you want to restore the previous version.

6 Click Restore.

Windows Vista restores the previous version.

7 Click OK.

8 Click OK.

TIPS

Did You Know?

Windows Vista also keeps track of previous versions of folders, which is useful if an entire folder becomes corrupted because of a system crash. Right-click the folder and then click Restore previous versions.

More Options!

If you are not sure which previous version to restore, click the previous version and then click Open to view the version. If you are still not sure, create a copy: Click the previous versions, click Copy, click a folder to store the copy, and then click Copy.

Chapter 5

Enhance Internet Security and Privacy

The Internet is now the online home away from home for hundreds of millions of people around the world. The lure of all that information, entertainment, and camaraderie has proven to be simply impossible to resist.

But the Internet has also lured more than its fair share of another class of people: malicious hackers, system intruders, and con artists of every stripe. These miscreants seem to spend most of their waking hours thinking up new ways to disrupt the Internet, break into your online computer, and steal everything from your credit card number to your full identity. Thankfully, such as crime in the real world, online crime is still relatively rare. However, as the newspaper headlines attest almost daily, cybercrime is a big business, and so it pays to play it safe.

This chapter helps by offering you a full suite of tasks and techniques designed to make your Internet sessions as safe as possible. You learn how to block specific Web sites; how to restrict Internet content; how to prevent a user from downloading files; how to scan your system for spyware; and how to use e-mail and Web media safely and securely.

Junk e-mail (spam) is a huge problem that is only getting worse, so you also learn in this chapter how to set up the Windows Mail junk e-mail protection feature.

Top 100

PROTECT CHILDREN
by activating parental controls

You can make computing safer for your children by activating the Windows Vista parental controls feature.

There are many aspects of computing that are not safe for young children. For example, the Web has many sites with material that is not suitable for young surfers. Similarly, many games have violent or mature content that should not be seen by children younger than a certain age.

You can restrict Web sites, games, and other content by activating the parental *controls* feature. Parental controls also enable you to set time limits on computer use and to view computer activity reports for your children.

Parental controls are also useful for keeping your computer safe from the activities of innocent or inexperienced users. For example, you can prevent children from downloading files, which might contain virus or other malicious programs.

Note that for parental controls to work, you must set up separate user accounts for the children who use your computer. When you create these accounts, make sure you set them up as Standard user accounts.

① Click Start.

② Click Control Panel.

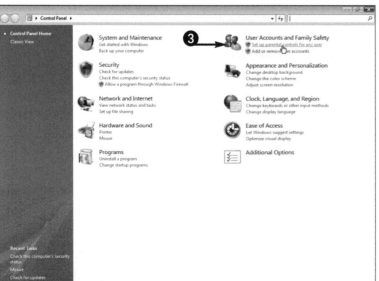

The Control Panel window appears.

③ Click Set up parental controls for any user.

Note: If the User Account Control dialog box appears, click Continue or type an administrator password and click Submit.

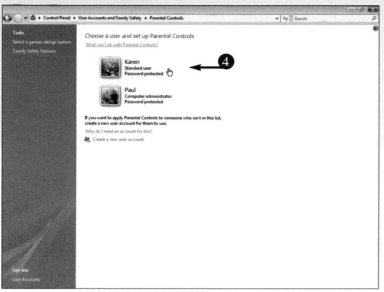

The Parental Controls window appears.

④ Click the user you want to control.

DIFFICULTY LEVEL

The User Controls window appears.

⑤ Click the On, enforce current settings option (○ changes to ⦿).

The Settings links become available.

⑥ Click the On, collect information about computer usage option (○ changes to ⦿).

⑦ Click the links in the Web Settings groups to configure controls for the user.

Note: See Task #43 to learn how to set up the Windows Vista Web Filter.

⑧ Click OK.

Windows Vista activates parental controls for the user.

More Options!

To restrict the times that the person can use the computer, click Time limits to display an hourly time grid. Click the hour blocks that you do not want the person to use the computer, and then click OK.

More Options!

To specify the programs the user can run, click Allow and block specific programs and then click the *User* can only use the programs I allow option (○ changes to ⦿). Click the check boxes beside the allowed programs (☐ changes to ☑), and then click OK.

More Options!

Windows Vista supports game ratings from the Entertainment Software Rating Board. To set the maximum game rating the person can play, click Games, click Set game ratings, click the maximum rating option (○ changes to ⦿), and then click OK.

AVOID OBJECTIONABLE MATERIAL
by filtering Web content

You can block objectionable material on the Web by configuring Windows Vista to not display certain Web sites and certain types of Web content for a particular person who uses your computer.

The World Wide Web is a vast resource that has a great deal of useful, entertaining, or interesting information. Plenty of material on the Web is suitable for all ages. However, unlike television, magazines, newspapers, and books, no one controls the content on the Web. Therefore, there are many sites that contain objectionable content.

If you share your computer with children, you can configure the Windows Vista Web Filter to block certain Web sites that you do not want those children to view. When a child attempts to view a blocked site, instead of displaying the site content, Internet Explorer displays a message that the site has been blocked. You can also filter Web content by setting up a restriction level or by blocking specific types of Web content.

Before performing the step in this section, be sure to activate parental controls (see Task #42).

① Open the User Controls window for the user you want to control.

Note: See Task #42 to learn how to display the User Controls window.

② Click Windows Vista Web Filter.

The Web Restrictions window appears.

③ Click Block some websites or content (○ changes to ⦿).

④ Click Edit the Allow block list.

The Allow Block Webpages window appears.

5 Type the address of a site you want to block.

6 Click Block.

● Windows Vista adds the address to the Blocked websites list.

7 Repeat steps **5** and **6** to block more sites.

8 Click OK.

43

DIFFICULTY LEVEL

9 Click the Custom option (◯ changes to ◉).

10 Click the check box for each Web content category that you want to block (☐ changes to ☑).

11 To block unrated sites, click the Unratable content check box (☐ changes to ☑).

12 To prevent the user from downloading files, click the Block file downloads check box (☐ changes to ☑).

13 Click OK.

Windows Vista puts the Web restrictions into effect.

More Options!

Rather than blocking specific Web sites, you can set up a more general *Web restriction level*. For example, to allow kids' only Web sites, click the High restriction option (◯ changes to ◉).

More Options!

For very young children, you may want to block off the entire Web except for sites you specify. To do this, click the Highest restriction option (◯ changes to ◉). Then click Allow or Block specific websites and for each allowed site, type its address and click Allow.

SCAN FOR SPYWARE
to remove malicious software

You can ensure that your computer is free of malicious software by scanning your computer for installed spyware.

One of the most common Internet-based threats to your computer is a type of software called spyware. *Spyware* refers to a program installed on your system without your knowledge to surreptitiously monitor your computer activities — particularly the typing of sensitive data, such as passwords, PINs, and credit card numbers — or to gather sensitive data from your computer. In both cases, the spyware then uses your Internet connection to send the collected data to an individual or company.

Most spyware programs install themselves without being bundled together with legitimate programs that you download from the Internet. Examples include file-sharing programs, download managers, and screen savers. After a spyware program is on your computer, it is generally extremely difficult to remove by hand. Instead, you need to use an antispyware program, such as Windows Defender, which comes with Windows Vista.

Scanning for spyware can take 20 minutes or more, so perform this task when you do not need to use your computer for a while.

❶ Click Start.

❷ Click All Programs.

❸ Click Windows Defender.

The Windows Defender window appears.

❹ Click the Scan menu.

❺ Click Full Scan.

Windows Defender begins the scan and displays the progress.

- If you need to interrupt the scan, click Stop Scan.

 # 44

DIFFICULTY LEVEL

- When the scan is complete, Windows Defender displays the results.

  Note: If Windows Defender finds any spyware, it displays a list of the programs. Follow the instructions on the screen to remove the spyware.

6 Click here to close Windows Defender.

TIPS

More Options!

By default, Windows Defender performs a Quick Scan of your computer every night at 2:00 AM if your computer is turned on. To run the more comprehensive Full Scan, instead, click Tools and then click Options. In the Type list, click Full system scan and then click Save.

Remove It!

If you prefer to use a third-party antispyware program, you should turn off Windows Defender. Click Tools and then click Options. At the bottom of the window, click the Use Windows Defender check box (☑ changes to ☐) and then click Save.

Play Web page media
SAFELY AND PRIVATELY

You can set options in Windows Media Player that ensure media downloaded from or played on an Internet site is safe and that enhance the privacy of the Internet media you play.

You can play Internet media either by downloading the music or video to your computer and playing it in Windows Media Player or by using a version of Windows Media Player that resides inside a Web page. Either way, the person who created the media may have included extra commands in a script that is

designed to control the playback. Unfortunately, scripts can also contain commands that can harm your computer, so preventing these scripts from running is the best option.

Also, Windows Media Player stores the names of media files that you play and the addresses of Web sites that you visit to access content. If other people use or have access to your computer, you may want to enhance your privacy by not allowing Windows Media Player to store this history.

❶ In Windows Media Player, click the Library tab's menu.

❷ Click More Options.

The Options dialog box appears.

❸ Click the Security tab.

❹ Click the Run script commands and rich media streams when the Player is in a Web page check box (☑ changes to ☐).

⑤ Click the Privacy tab.

⑥ Click the Save file and URL history in the Player check box (☑ changes to ☐).

⑦ Click OK.

Windows Media Player puts the new security and privacy options into effect.

TIPS

More Options!

Some media sites display *enhanced content*, or Web pages that give you information related to the media. Because these pages can contain malicious content, Media Player asks if you want to see the enhanced content. If you trust your sites, bypass this prompt by displaying the Security tab and clicking the Play enhanced content that uses Web pages without prompting check box (☐ changes to ☑).

Important!

Some content sites require a Player ID before you can play any media. For example, a site may request the ID for billing purposes. In that case, enable Media Player to send the ID by displaying the Privacy tab and clicking the Send unique Player ID to content providers check box (☐ changes to ☑).

Set the junk e-mail protection level to
AVOID SPAM

You can configure the Windows Mail junk e-mail protection level to strike a balance between avoiding spam and missing important non-spam messages.

When setting the junk e-mail protection level in Windows Mail, your goal should be to find a level that flags the most spam and the fewest false positives — legitimate messages flagged as spam. To help you do this, Windows Mail offers four protection levels:

The No Automatic Filtering level turns off the junk e-mail filter. Choose this option only if you use another junk e-mail filter or receive no junk e-mail.

The Low level flags only messages with obvious spam content. Choose this option if you get only a few junk e-mails each day.

The High level handles spam aggressively, so it almost never misses a junk e-mail, but it also generates regular false positives. Choose this level if you get a few dozen junk e-mails each day.

The Safe Lists Only level treats all incoming messages as spam, except for messages from people in your Safe Senders list (see Task #47). Use this level if you get a hundred or more junk e-mails each day.

① Click Start.

② Click E-mail.

The Windows Mail window appears.

③ Click Tools.

④ Click Junk E-mail Options.

The Junk E-mail Options dialog box appears.

⑤ Click the junk e-mail protection level option you want to use (○ changes to ◉).

⑥ Click the Phishing tab.

⑦ Click the Move phishing E-mail to the Junk Mail folder check box (☐ changes to ☑).

⑧ Click OK.

Windows Mail puts the new settings into effect.

Did You Know?

A *phishing* e-mail is a message that pretends to be from a legitimate business or organization. The message includes links that take you to a Web site where you are asked to provide a password, credit card data, or other sensitive information.

Reverse It!

If you select the High level of junk e-mail protection, be sure to check the Junk E-mail folder regularly to look for false positives. If you get a false positive in your Junk E-mail folder, click the message and then click Message, Junk E-mail, Mark as Not Junk. Windows Mail returns the message to the Inbox folder.

Add a person to your
BLOCKED SENDERS LIST

If you receive spam or other unwanted messages from a particular person, you can configure Windows Mail to block that person's address so that you do not have to see or deal with messages from that person again.

Spam messages are most often sent with fake return addresses that change with each message. However, it often happens that a particular person sends junk messages using a legitimate return e-mail address. In this case, you can add that address to the Windows Mail Blocked Senders list. Any future

messages from that person — as well as any messages from that person currently in your Inbox folder — are automatically rerouted to the Junk E-mail folder.

However, the Blocked Senders list is not just for spam. If you have a person who is sending you annoying, insulting, or offensive messages, you can add that person's address to the Blocked Senders list. Again, Windows Mail automatically moves that person's messages to the Junk E-mail folder so you do not have to deal with them.

① In Windows Mail, click Tools.

② Click Junk E-mail Options.

The Junk E-mail Options dialog box appears.

③ Click the Blocked Senders tab.

④ Click Add.

The Add address or domain dialog box appears.

⑤ Type the address of the person you want to block.

⑥ Click OK.

● Windows Mail adds the address to the Blocked Senders list.

⑦ Repeat steps **4** to **6** to add more addresses to your Blocked Senders list.

⑧ Click OK.

If any of the people you added to the Blocked Senders list have messages in your Inbox folder, Windows Mail moves those messages to the Junk E-mail folder.

Try This!

Some spammers use varying addresses that change the user name but keep the same domain name — for example, sales@spammer.com, offers@spammer.com, and so on. To block all messages from this type of spammer, add just the domain name — spammer.com in this example — to the Blocked Senders list.

More Options!

If you have a message from a person you want to block, click the message, click Message, and then click Junk E-mail. In the menu that appears, click either Add Sender to Blocked Senders List or Add Sender's Domain to Blocked Senders List.

BLOCK MESSAGES FROM A COUNTRY

to reduce spam

If you receive a great deal of spam from e-mail addresses that originate in a particular country, you can avoid dealing with those messages by telling Windows Mail to block messages that come from that country.

On the Internet, a *top-level domain name* is a domain name with any other qualifier added. Many of these top-level domain names end with domain codes, such as .com, .edu, and .org that are not country-specific. However, many top-level domains

do use country or region codes. For example, .ca is the domain code for Canada, .uk is for Great Britain, .de is for Germany, and .us is for the United States.

If you find that you are getting many spam messages from addresses that use a domain code for a particular country, you can configure Windows Mail to block messages from such domains. Any future messages from that country are automatically moved to the Junk E-mail folder.

① In Windows Mail, click Tools.

② Click Junk E-mail Options.

The Junk E-mail Options dialog box appears.

③ Click the International tab.

④ Click Blocked Top-Level Domain List.

The Blocked Top-Level Domain List dialog box appears.

⑤ Click the check box for each country you want to block (☐ changes to ☑).

⑥ Click OK.

⑦ Click OK.

Windows Mail begins blocking messages from the country or countries you selected.

If any of the messages in your Inbox folder come from the blocked countries, Windows Mail moves those messages to the Junk E-mail folder.

TIPS

More Options!
If you want to block messages from all foreign countries with just a few exceptions, activating most of the check boxes in the Blocked Top-Level Domain dialog box can be time-consuming. An easier method is to click Select All to activate every check box and then click to uncheck the countries you do not want blocked (☑ changes to ☐).

Try This!
If you regularly get messages written in a different language that you do not understand, you should treat such messages as junk e-mail. To configure Windows Mail to block such messages, follow steps **1** to **3** and then click Blocked Encoding List. In the Blocked Encodings List dialog box, click the check box for each language you want to block (☐ changes to ☑), and then click OK.

Add a person to your
SAFE SENDERS LIST

If you only want to receive e-mail messages from a particular group of people, you can add those people to your Safe Senders list. Windows Mail will block all other incoming messages.

If you have set the junk e-mail protection level (see Task #46), are blocking the addresses of known spammers (see Task #47), and have blocked spam that originates in some countries (see Task #48), then you should have your spam problem under control.

However, if you find that you are still receiving too much junk e-mail, then it may be time for you to try the opposite approach. That is, instead of trying to block spam using so-called *black lists*, you can configure Windows Mail to allow only mail from addresses that you specify — a *white list* that Windows Mail calls the Safe Senders list. This method virtually eliminates spam from getting to you because it is unlikely that any spammer will use a spoof address that corresponds to any address in your Safe Senders list.

① In Windows Mail, click Tools.

② Click Junk E-mail Options.

The Junk E-mail Options dialog box appears.

③ Click the Safe Senders tab.

④ Click Add.

The Add address or domain dialog box appears.

⑤ Type the address of the person from whom you want to receive messages.

⑥ Click OK.

● Windows Mail adds the address to the Safe Senders list.

⑦ Repeat steps **4** to **6** to add more addresses to your Safe Senders list.

⑧ Click OK.

Try This!

If you correspond with several people who work for a particular company, you do not need to add each person's address to your Safe Senders list. Instead, you can save time by adding just the company's domain name to the Safe Senders list. That way, you see all the messages that come from that company, even from people you have never corresponded with in the past.

More Options!

If you have a message from a person you want add to your Safe Senders list, click the message, click Message, and then click Junk E-mail. In the menu that appears, click either Add Sender to Safe Senders List or Add Sender's Domain to Safe Senders List.

Prevent Windows Mail from
SENDING A READ RECEIPT

You can block Windows Mail from sending a message that confirms you have opened a message.

The Internet e-mail system occasionally breaks down and some e-mail messages never arrive at their destination. Often you get no indication that there was a problem, so you assume the message got through.

A person sending an important message may want to know whether you have read the message because then at least they know the message was delivered safely. A *read receipt* is a short message that Windows Mail automatically fires back to the sender

when you open or preview a message from that person. The read receipt — which must be requested by the sender — ensures the sender that you have viewed the message. However, many people consider this an invasion of privacy, so they block Windows Mail from sending read receipts.

By default, Windows Mail displays a dialog box that tells you the sender has requested a read receipt. You can block read receipts either by declining to send one each time Windows Mail asks or by blocking read receipts entirely.

PREVENT A SINGLE READ RECEIPT

● This dialog box appears when the sender requests a read receipt.

❶ Click No.

PREVENT ALL READ RECEIPTS

❶ In Windows Mail, click Tools.

❷ Click Options.

The Options dialog box appears.

③ Click the Receipts tab.

④ Click the Never send a read receipt option (◯ changes to ⦿).

⑤ Click OK.

Windows Mail stops sending read receipts to confirm that you have read e-mail.

TIPS

More Options!
You may find that read receipts are useful in business. For example, if someone sends you an important message, it is easier to confirm that you have received the message by having Windows Mail send a read receipt than sending a response yourself. In that case, click the Notify me for each read receipt request option (◯ changes to ⦿). This enables you to control when you send a read receipt.

More Options!
If you do not mind that other people know when you read a message, you may not want to be bothered with the read receipt dialog box each time a request comes in. In that case, click the Always send a read receipt option (◯ changes to ⦿).

Configure Windows Mail to
THWART E-MAIL VIRUSES

You can reduce the danger of accidentally unleashing a virus on your computer by reading all your e-mail messages in text format.

E-mail messages come in two formats: plain text and HTML. The plain text format just uses the letters, numbers, and symbols that you can type on your keyboard. It contains no fonts, colors, images, or other formatting.

The HTML format utilizes the same codes that are used to create Web pages. This means that HTML messages can use different fonts and colors, they

can insert lines and images, and they can use any of the other formatting that you see on Web pages.

However, you may know that some Web pages are unsafe because they can contain malicious scripts that can cause problems on your computer. Unfortunately, this also means that HTML formatted e-mail messages also have the potential to be unsafe because they may contain virus scripts that run automatically when you open or even just preview a message. You can prevent these scripts from running by viewing all your messages in the plain text format.

① In Windows Mail, click Tools.

② Click Options.

The Options dialog box appears.

③ Click the Read tab.

④ Click the Read all messages in plain text check box (☐ changes to ☑).

51

⑤ Click OK.

Windows Mail displays all messages in plain text instead of HTML.

Did You Know?

When you are viewing a message as plain text, you may realize that the message is innocuous and that it is okay to view the HTML version. To switch quickly to HTML, click View and then click Message in HTML. You can also press Alt+Shift+H.

More Options!

Windows Mail has several other options that thwart viruses. They are usually activated by default, but you should make sure of this. In the Options dialog box, click the Security tab. Click the Restricted sites zone option (◯ changes to ◉), and the Warn me when other applications try to send mail as me and Do not allow attachments to be saved or opened that could potentially be a virus check boxes (☐ changes to ☑).

Unleash the Power
of Internet Explorer

The World Wide Web is arguably the most impressive of the various services accessible via the Internet. With *billions* of pages available covering practically every imaginable topic, the Web is one of our greatest inventions and an unparalleled source of information.

One problem with the Web, though, is actually getting at all that information. With so much online ground to cover, you want a reliable and efficient means of transportation. For the World Wide Web, the vehicle of choice is the Web browser, and in Windows XP, the default Web browser is Internet Explorer. This program is fairly easy to use if all you do is click links and type Web site addresses. But to get the

most out of the Web, you can tap into the impressive array of features and options that Internet Explorer offers.

This chapter helps you do just that by taking you through a few truly useful tips and tricks that unleash the power of Internet Explorer. You learn how to take advantage of the new tabs in the Windows Vista version of Internet Explorer; subscribe to Web feeds; use your favorite search engine with Internet Explorer; search for Web sites directly from the Internet Explorer Address bar; clear Address bar addresses to maintain the privacy of your surfing; and view pop-up windows for specific sites.

Top 100

Save time by automatically
SWITCHING TO NEW TABS

You can make the Internet Explorer tab feature much more convenient by configuring the program to automatically switch to new tabs as you create them. In previous versions of Internet Explorer, if you wanted to open multiple Web sites at once, you had to open multiple copies of the Internet Explorer window. It was not unusual for users to have a half a dozen or more Internet Explorer windows open at once, which was confusing and cluttered the desktop and taskbar.

The new version of Internet Explorer that comes with Windows Vista supports *tabbed browsing*, which means you can open multiple Web sites at once in a single browser window. Each site appears in its own tab, and you can switch from one site to another just by clicking the tabs.

To open a site in a new tab, you right-click the link and then click Open in New Tab. Internet Explorer creates the tab and then opens the Web page in the tab. However, to see the page, you must then click the tab.

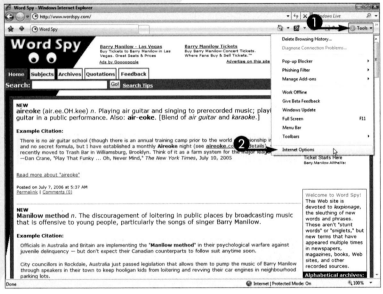

① Click Tools.

② Click Internet Options.

The Internet Options dialog box appears.

③ Click the General tab.

④ In the Tabs group, click Settings.

The Tabbed Browsing Settings dialog box appears.

⑤ Click the Always switch to new tabs when they are created check box (☐ changes to ☑).

⑥ Click OK.

⑦ Click OK.

TIPS

Did You Know?

A quicker method to open a link in a new tab is to hold down Ctrl when you click the link. You can also open sites from the Address bar in a new tab. To do this, type the address and then press Alt+Enter.

More Options!

When you create a new tab by clicking the New Tab button or pressing Ctrl+T, Internet Explorer displays a blank page. To load your home page, instead, follow steps **1** to **4**, click the Open home page for new tabs instead of a blank page check box (☐ changes to ☑), and then click OK.

View open pages as
QUICK TABS

You can easily view and switch between the Web pages open in your tabs by using the Internet Explorer Quick Tabs feature. Opening multiple pages in a single Internet Explorer window using tabs is convenient. However, tabs do suffer from one drawback. Depending on the width of your monitor and the screen resolution you are using, Internet Explorer can display only a limited number of tabs. For example, a typical monitor running 800 × 600 screen resolution can display a maximum of five tabs.

If you have more tabs open than Internet Explorer can display, the program adds arrow buttons to scroll left and right through the tabs. But scrolling is not always convenient because each tab gives you only a minimum amount of information.

When you are dealing with a large number of tabs, a faster way to navigate the tabs is to use the Internet Explorer Quick Tabs feature, which displays a thumbnail image of each open Web page. You can then click the thumbnail of the page you want to immediately switch to that tab.

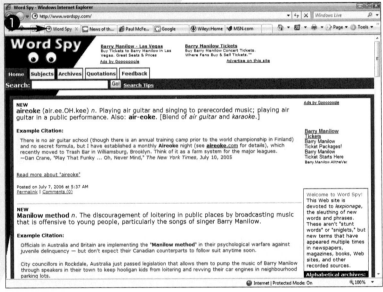

① Open pages in two or more tabs.

② Click the Quick Tabs button.

Note: You can also select the Quick Tabs button by pressing Ctrl+Q.

Internet Explorer
displays thumbnail
images of the Web
pages in each tab.

③ Click the Web page
you want to view.

53

DIFFICULTY LEVEL

Internet Explorer switches to the tab that
contains the Web page you selected.

TIPS

More Options!

Internet Explorer also maintains a Tab
List, which is a list of the names of the
Web pages you have open in the current
Internet Explorer window. To display the
Tab List, click the drop-down arrow to
the right of the Quick Tabs button. (Note
that you can only display the Tab List if
you have at least two tabs open.) You
can then click a page name to switch to
that tab.

Remove It!

If you find that you do not use the Quick
Tabs feature, you can turn it off to make
room for more tabs. Click Tools and
then click Internet Options to display
the Internet Options dialog box. In the
General tab, click Settings in the Tabs
group and then click the Enable Quick
Tabs check box (☑ changes to ☐).
Click OK in the open dialog boxes and
then restart Internet Explorer.

OPEN MULTIPLE PAGES
when you start Internet Explorer

If you regularly view several different pages at the start of each Internet Explorer session, you can save time by opening those pages automatically each time you start Internet Explorer.

In Internet Explorer, the *home page* is the page that the browser displays automatically when you first start the program. The default Internet Explorer home page is Live.com, but most people change that to a page that they use regularly.

However, you may have more than one page that you open after Internet Explorer starts. For example,

you may open a portal page such as MSN or Yahoo, a search page such as Google, your company's external or internal Web site, a news page, one or more blogger pages, and so on. Opening each new tab and navigating to the appropriate page can take time.

The Windows Vista version of Internet Explorer enables you to define multiple home pages. Internet Explorer automatically opens each home page in its own tab when you launch the program.

① Open the Web page that you want to add as a home page.

② Click the Home menu.

③ Click Add or Change Home Page.

The Add or Change Home Page dialog box appears.

④ Click the **Add this webpage to your home page tabs** option (○ changes to ◉).

⑤ Click **Yes**.

● Internet Explorer adds the page to the Home list.

More Options!

If you do not currently have access to the Internet, you can still add a site as a home page. Click Tools and then click Internet Options to display the Internet Options dialog box. In the General tab, click the last item in the Home page list, press End, and then press Enter to start a new line. Type the address of the new home page and then click OK.

Remove It!

If you have set up a site as one of your Internet Explorer home pages, but you no longer visit that site, you should remove it to reduce the time it takes for Internet Explorer to launch. Click the Home menu, click Remove, and then click the home page that you want to delete. When Internet Explorer asks you to confirm, click Yes.

SUBSCRIBE TO A WEB FEED
to see new site content

You can keep up-to-date with a Web site by subscribing to its Web feed, which displays the latest site content. Some Web sites remain relatively static over time, so you only need to check in every once in a while to see if anything is new. Some Web sites change content regularly, such as once a day or once a week, so you know in advance when to check for new material. However, there are many sites — particularly Web logs, or blogs — where the content changes frequently, although not at a regular interval. For these sites, keeping up with new content

can be time-consuming, and it is easy to miss new information.

To solve this problem, many Web sites now maintain Web feeds, which are also called RSS feeds (RSS stands for Real Simple Syndication). A *Web feed* is a special file that contains the most recent information added to the site. You can use Internet Explorer to subscribe to a site's Web feed. This makes it easy to view the feed any time you like to see the site's new content.

① Navigate to the site with which you want to work.

● If the site has at least one Web feed, the Feeds button becomes activated.

② Click the drop-down arrow to display the Feeds list.

③ Click the feed you want to view.

Internet Explorer displays the feed.

④ Click Subscribe to this feed.

The Subscribe to this Feed dialog box appears.

⑤ Type a new name for the feed (this is optional).

⑥ Click Subscribe.

Internet Explorer subscribes to the feed.

55

DIFFICULTY LEVEL

VIEW A FEED

① Click Favorites Center.

② Click Feeds.

● Internet Explorer displays the feeds.

Note: You can also display the Feeds list by pressing Ctrl+J.

③ Click the feed you want to view.

TIPS

More Options!

Internet Explorer activates the Feeds button when it finds a feed on a site. If you want a stronger indication that a feed is available, click Tools then click Internet Options to display the Internet Options dialog box. Click the Content tab and then click Settings in the Feeds group. Click the Play a sound when a feed is found for a webpage check box (☐ changes to ☑). Click OK.

Remove It!

If you no longer want to view the feed from a particular site, you should delete the feed to reduce the clutter in your Feeds list. Click Favorites Center and then click Feeds to display your subscribed feeds. Right-click the feed you want to remove and then click Delete. When Internet Explorer asks you to confirm, click Yes.

Set the
WEB FEED REFRESH FREQUENCY

You can customize the frequency with which Internet Explorer refreshes a Web feed to suit the way you work or the nature of the feed.

With most Web sites that offer a feed, the feed is updated at the same time as, or soon after, new content is posted to the site. The frequency with which this occurs varies widely: once a day, once a week, several times a day, or even several times an hour.

By default, Internet Explorer checks for an updated feed once per day. This is a reasonable schedule for a site that posts new content once or twice a day or every couple of days. However, it is not an efficient schedule for feeds that are updated much more or much less frequently. If a feed updates only once a week, checking the feed every day is wasteful for Internet Explorer. You can make a feed more efficient or easier to read by setting up a custom refresh schedule that suits the feed.

❶ Click Favorites Center.

❷ Click Feeds.

❸ Right-click the feed you want to view.

❹ Click Properties.

The Feed Properties
dialog box appears.

5 Click the Use custom
schedule option
(◯ changes to ◉).

DIFFICULTY LEVEL

6 Click the Frequency list drop-down arrow.

7 Click the frequency with which you want
to check the feed.

8 Click OK.

Internet Explorer updates the feed's
refresh frequency.

TIPS

Did You Know?

How can you tell whether a feed has new
posts? The easiest method is to click the
Favorites Center button and then click Feeds.
If Internet Explorer displays a feed's title in
bold text, it means the feed has new posts.
Note, too, that when you hover the mouse
pointer over a feed, Internet Explorer displays
the Refresh this Feed button on the right side
of the Feeds pane. Click that button to have
Internet Explorer check for new feeds.

More Options!

The default interval that Internet Explorer uses
to check feeds for new posts is once a day. To
change the default schedule, click Tools, then
click Internet Options to display the Internet
Options dialog box. Click the Content tab and
then click Settings in the Feeds group. Use the
Default schedule list to click the interval you
want to use, and then click OK.

Improve searching by
ADDING SEARCH ENGINES

You can make your Web searches more powerful by adding your favorite search engines to the Internet Explorer Search box.

With billions of pages, the World Wide Web is an amazing information resource. However, it can also be a frustrating resource because *finding* the page you want among those billions is a real challenge. You can ask friends and family, or you can use a site such as Yahoo.com that categorizes pages, but these strategies are often unreliable.

To find the site you want, you can take advantage of the various search engines that enable you to find

Web pages based on the search text you provide. The Internet Explorer Search box uses the Live Search site to perform its searches.

If you have a search engine other than Live Search that you prefer above all others, you may decide that it is worth the extra effort to navigate to that site rather than using Live Search via the Internet Explorer Search box. However, you can have it both ways. You can configure Internet Explorer to use your favorite search engine via the Search box.

① Click the Search menu.

② Click Find More Providers.

The Add Search Providers to Internet Explorer 7 Web page appears.

③ Click the search engine you want to add to Internet Explorer 7.

The Add Search Provider dialog box appears.

④ Click Add Provider.

Internet Explorer adds the search engine.

⑤ Click the Search menu.

● The new search engine appears in the Search list. Click the search engine to use it with the Search box.

TIPS

More Options!

The search engine that Internet Explorer uses in the Search box when you first start the program is called the *default search provider*. The default is Live Search, but you can change it to one of your added search engines. Click the Search menu and then click Change Search Defaults. In the Change Search Defaults dialog box, click the search engine you want to use and then click Set Default. Click OK.

Remove It!

If you add a search engine and later decide you do not want to use it, you should delete it to avoid cluttering the Search list. To remove a search engine, click the Search menu and then click Change Search Defaults. In the Change Search Defaults dialog box, click the search engine you want to delete and then click Remove. Click OK.

CUSTOMIZE THE LINKS BAR
for easier surfing

You can customize the Internet Explorer Links bar to provide easy one-click access to those Web sites that you visit most often. If you have Web sites that you visit often, adding them to the Internet Explorer Favorites list is a good idea so that you have an easy-to-access list of your regular sites.

For sites that you visit constantly, the few clicks that it requires to load the sites from the Favorites menu can begin to seem inefficient. For even faster site access, consider the Links bar. This is one of the

most useful features of Internet Explorer, but paradoxically it is also one of its most hidden. The Links bar — which is turned off, by default — is a toolbar that is designed to hold a collection of buttons, each of which is associated with a Web site. When you click a button, Internet Explorer automatically navigates to the associated site. This gives you one-click access to those sites you visit most often.

DISPLAY THE LINKS BAR

① Right-click an empty section of the Internet Explorer toolbar.

② Click Links.

● Internet Explorer displays the Links bar.

CREATE A BUTTON FOR THE CURRENT WEB PAGE

❶ Navigate to the page with which you want to work.

❷ Click and drag the Address bar icon and drop it on the Links bar.

● A new button associated with the page appears on the Links bar. You can click this button to navigate directly to the page.

CREATE A BUTTON FROM A WEB PAGE LINK

❶ Navigate to the page that contains the link with which you want to work.

❷ Click and drag the link text and drop it on the Links bar.

● A new button associated with the linked page appears on the Links bar. You can click this button to navigate directly to the linked page.

TIPS

Customize It!

The positions of the Links bar buttons are not fixed. To move a button to another position, click and drag the button and then drop it in the position you prefer. To rename a button, right-click it, click Rename, type the new name in the Rename dialog box, and then click OK. To delete a button, right-click it, click Delete, and then click Yes when Windows Vista asks you to confirm.

Did You Know?

If the address of one of your sites changes, you can edit the address associated with the site's Links bar button. Right-click the button and then click Properties. In the button's Properties dialog box, type the new address in the URL text box. Click OK.

SAVE WEB SITES LONGER
to surf more efficiently

You can improve the efficiency of your Web surfing by increasing the number of days that Internet Explorer maintains a record of the sites you have visited. When you navigate to a Web page, Internet Explorer adds the page's title and address to the History list, which is part of the Favorites Center. The History list is an important Internet Explorer feature because it enables you to easily and quickly return to a page that you have previously visited. The History list also enables you to view the pages that you have visited most often, so it gives you an easy way to see which pages are your favorites.

By default, Internet Explorer keeps a page in the History list for 20 days before removing it. However, you may find that you often want to revisit pages after the 20-day period has expired. In that case, you can configure Internet Explorer to save pages in the History list for a longer period. The maximum number of days you can save pages is 999.

❶ Click Tools.

❷ Click Internet Options.

The Internet Options dialog box appears.

❸ In the Browsing history group, click Settings.

The Temporary Internet Files and History Settings dialog box appears.

④ Use the Days to keep pages in history spin box to type or click the number of days you want Web sites saved.

⑤ Click OK.

⑥ Click OK.

Internet Explorer puts the new setting into effect.

TIPS

Try This!

To work with the History list, click the Favorites Center button and then click History. (You can also press Ctrl+H.) The History list organizes your visited sites into date categories such as Today, Yesterday, Last Week, and Last Month. Click a category, click the site with which you want to work, and then click the specific page you want to visit.

Did You Know?

You can sort the History list in various ways. The default sort order is By Date. To change this, display the Favorites Center, click the History menu, and then click By Site, By Most Visited, or By Order Visited Today. You can also click Search History to perform a search on the history entries.

DELETE YOUR BROWSING HISTORY
to ensure privacy

To ensure that other people who have access to your computer cannot view information from sites you have visited, you can delete your browsing history. As you visit Web sites, Internet Explorer maintains information about the sites you visit. Internet Explorer also maintains a folder called Temporary Internet Files which stores copies of page text, images, and other content so that sites load faster the next time you view them. Similarly, Internet Explorer also saves text and passwords that you have typed into forms. Internet Explorer also maintains *cookies*, which are small text files that

store information such as site preferences and site log on data.

Saving all this data is useful because it enables you to quickly revisit a site. However, it is also dangerous because other people who use your computer can just as easily visit or view information about those sites. This can be a problem if you visit financial sites, private corporate sites, or some other page that you would not want another person to visit. You reduce this risk by deleting some or all of your browsing history.

1 Click Tools.

2 Click Delete Browsing History.

The Delete Browsing History dialog box appears.

3 To delete a specific part of your browsing history, click the appropriate button.

Internet Explorer asks you to confirm.

④ Click Yes.

Internet Explorer deletes the specified browsing history.

⑤ Repeats steps **3** and **4** to delete other parts of your browsing history.

⑥ To delete all of your browsing history, click Delete all.

Internet Explorer asks you to confirm.

⑦ Click Yes.

Internet Explorer deletes all the browsing history and closes the Delete Browsing History dialog box.

● If you did not delete all your browsing history, click Close to exit the Delete Browsing History dialog box.

TIPS

More Options!

You can control whether Internet Explorer saves your form data as well as your site user names and passwords. Click Tools and then click Internet Options to display the Internet Options dialog box. Click the Content tab and then click Settings in the AutoComplete group. In the AutoComplete Settings dialog box, click to uncheck Forms to stop saving form data. Click to uncheck User names and passwords on forms to stop saving log on data. Click OK.

Did You Know?

The Internet Explorer Address bar also doubles as a drop-down list. Click the Address bar drop-down arrow and you see a list of the last few addresses that you have typed into the Address bar text box. However, when you delete the contents of the History list, you also delete the items in the Address bar list.

VIEW POP-UP ADS
from a specific Web site

You can improve your surfing experience by configuring Internet Explorer to view the pop-up ads for certain Web sites that Internet Explorer would otherwise block.

Web page advertising is a necessary evil because Web masters often need the money from advertisers to help defray the inevitable costs of maintaining a site. Banner ads are a popular choice, but to make more of an impact, advertisers often insist that their ads appear in separate pop-up windows. These pop-ups are everywhere on the Web these days. Small personal pages may display a single pop-up

when you enter or leave the site; some commercial sites display a few pop-ups as you peruse their pages; and then there are those sites that throw out a barrage of pop-ups. Depending on your level of tolerance, pop-ups are either mildly irritating or downright annoying. Either way, pop-up ads can make surfing the Web a real chore.

However, some sites display useful information in pop-up windows, and Internet Explorer may block these windows. If so, you can add the site's address to the list of sites that are allowed to display pop-ups.

① Click Tools.

② Click Pop-up Blocker.

③ Click Pop-up Blocker Settings.

The Pop-up Blocker Settings dialog box appears.

④ Type that site address in the Address of website to allow text box.

⑤ Click Add.

- Internet Explorer includes the address in the Allowed sites list.

6 Repeat steps **4** and **5** to add other sites to the Allowed sites list.

7 Click Close.

8 Restart Internet Explorer.

The next time you visit the site, Internet Explorer displays its pop-up windows.

TIPS

More Options!

Rather than typing a site's address in the Pop-up Blocker Settings dialog box, an easier method is to navigate to the site and look for the Internet Explorer Information Bar that appears when the program blocks a pop-up. Click the Information Bar, click Always Allow Pop-ups from This Site, and then click Yes when Internet Explorer asks you to confirm.

More Options!

If you only want to occasionally allow pop-ups from a site, follow steps **1** to **3**, use the Filter Level list to click High: Block all pop-ups, and then click OK. The next time you navigate to the site and want to view its pop-ups, hold down Ctrl and Alt until the pop-up appears.

Chapter 7

Make E-Mail Easier

The World Wide Web may be the most impressive of the Internet services, but it would not be hard to make the case that e-mail is the most indispensable. E-mail, which most of us have been using for only a few years, leaves us wondering how we ever managed without it. E-mail's position midway between conversation and letter writing makes it ideal for certain types of communication, and rarely can a person be found nowadays who does not rely on it.

The fact that e-mail is easy to use also helps. Even novice computer users seem to grasp the basic e-mail idea quickly and are often sending messages within minutes. But if, like most people, you use e-mail all day long, you probably want to make it even easier. This chapter shows you how to do that. The tasks you learn here are designed to save precious seconds and minutes of everyday e-mail chores. That may not sound like much, but added up over the course of a busy e-mail day, those seconds can make the difference between leaving work on time and staying late.

Among the timesavers in this chapter, you learn how to leave messages on the server; how to change your message priority; how to create an e-mail distribution list; how to create a backup copy of your address book; how to exchange electronic business cards; and how to spell check your messages.

Top 100

LEAVE YOUR MESSAGES
on the server

You can configure Windows Mail to leave your messages on the server, enabling you to retrieve a message multiple times from different computers. When you ask Windows Mail to retrieve your messages, it contacts your Internet service provider's e-mail server, downloads the messages, and then deletes them from the server. However, there may be times when you do not want the messages deleted. It is better to leave them on the server so that you can also retrieve them when you return to the office.

DIFFICULTY LEVEL

TIP

More Options!
Most ISPs offer a limited amount of e-mail storage space, so you cannot leave messages on the server indefinitely. To ensure that your messages are deleted eventually, follow steps **1** to **5** and then click the Remove from server after *x* days check box (☐ changes to ☑), where *x* is the number of days after which you want the server messages deleted.

① In Windows Mail, click Tools.

② Click Accounts.

The Internet Accounts dialog box appears.

③ Click the account with which you want to work.

④ Click Properties.

⑤ In the account's Properties dialog box, click the Advanced tab.

⑥ Click the Leave a copy of messages on server check box (☐ changes to ☑).

⑦ Click OK.

⑧ Click Close.

Windows Mail leaves a copy of the messages on the server.

Change your MESSAGE PRIORITY

You can set the priority level of your outgoing message to let the recipient know whether to handle your message with high or low priority.

If you are sending a message that has important information or that requires a fast response, set the message's priority to high. When the recipient receives the message, Windows Mail indicates a high priority messages with a red exclamation mark. Alternatively, you can set the priority to low for unimportant messages so that the recipient knows not to handle the message immediately. Windows Mail flags low priority messages with a blue, downward-pointing arrow.

Did You Know?

If you are sending important information via e-mail, you may want to ensure that the message arrived safely. You can do that by sending a request for a read receipt, which is a message that is automatically sent to you when the recipient reads the message for the first time. In the message window, click Tools and then click Request Read Receipt.

① In Windows Mail, click File.

② Click New.

③ Click Mail Message.

Note: You can also click Create Mail in the toolbar.

The New Message window appears.

④ Click Message.

⑤ Click Set Priority.

⑥ Click the priority you want to use.

● You can also click Priority in the toolbar.

● When you choose High or Low priority, Windows Mail indicates the current priority level.

E-MAIL MULTIPLE PEOPLE
using a contact group

If you regularly send messages to a particular collection of people, you can organize those recipients into a group. This saves time because when you choose the group as the message recipient, Windows Mail sends the message to every address in the group.

Sending a message to a number of people takes time because you have to either type many addresses or select many people from your address book. If you find that you are sending some of your messages to the same group repeatedly, you can avoid the

drudgery of adding those recipients individually by creating a distribution list or, as Windows Mail calls it, a *contact group*.

After you add the recipients to the list, all you have to do is send the message to the group. Windows Mail then distributes copies of the message to every member of the group. An added benefit is that recipients do not see the names or addresses of the other group members so maintaining group privacy is easy.

① In Windows Mail, click Tools.

② Click Windows Contacts.

● You can also click the Contacts toolbar button, or press Ctrl+Shift+C.

The Contacts window appears.

③ Click New Contact Group.

The group's Properties dialog box appears.

#64

DIFFICULTY LEVEL

④ Use the Group Name text box to type the name of the group.

⑤ Use the Contact Name text box to type the name of a person you want to add to the group.

⑥ Use the E-mail text box to type the person's e-mail address.

⑦ Click Create for Group Only.

⑧ Repeat steps **5** to **7** to add other members of the group.

⑨ Click OK.

● The group name appears in the Contacts window.

Note: If you do not see the group at first, press F5 to refresh the Contacts window.

⑩ Click the Close button to close the Contacts window.

TIPS

More Options!

If some or all of the people you want to add to the group are already listed in your Contacts list, you can use an easier method to add them to the group. In the group's Properties dialog box, click Add to Contact Group to open the Add Members to Contact Group dialog box. For each person you want to add, hold down Ctrl and click the person's name. Click Add when you are done.

More Options!

You can add a person to your group *and* add him or her to your Contacts list at the same time. In the group's Properties dialog box, click Create New Contact. Type the person's name in the First and Last text boxes and the persons' e-mail address in the E-mail text box, and then click OK. Windows Mail adds the person to your group and to your Contacts list.

PROTECT YOUR CONTACTS
by creating a backup copy

You can create a backup copy of your Contacts. If you have a problem with the Contacts in the future, you can restore your contacts from the backup copy.

The Windows Vista Contacts folder is handy for storing e-mail addresses of people you correspond with regularly. Instead of remembering complex e-mail addresses, you simply type or select the person's name when composing a new message. However, the usefulness of the Contacts folder extends far beyond e-mail. For each contact, you can also store data such as his or her home and business

addresses, phone, fax, and cell numbers, spouse and children's names, gender, birthday, and more.

If you rely on the Contacts folder to store all this information about the people you know, then you must ensure that the data is safe. Unfortunately, Contacts is just a folder on your hard drive, and if that folder gets corrupted, you could lose all your contact data. Just in case this happens, you can regularly create backup copies of your Contacts folder.

---

① In Windows Mail, click File.

② Click Export.

③ Click Windows Contacts.

The Export Windows Contacts dialog box appears.

④ Click CSV (Comma Separated Values).

⑤ Click Export.

The CSV Export dialog box appears.

⑥ Type the location and name of the exported file.

*Note: Be sure to add **.csv** to the end of the exported filename.*

⑦ Click Next.

8 Click the check boxes for each field you want to include (☑) or exclude (☐).

9 Click Finish.

Windows Mail exports the Address Book data to the file.

● The progress of the export is shown here.

⑩ When the export is complete, click OK.

⑪ Click Close.

Important!

If you have a problem with your Contacts folder — for example, if it does not open or does not display your contacts — you can restore it by importing the backed-up copy. In Windows Mail, click File, Import, and then Windows Contacts. Click CSV (Comma Separated Values), and then click Import. Type the location and name of the exported file from step **6** and click Next. Click Finish.

Did You Know!

If you prefer to create a backup copy of the actual Contacts folder, you must first open your user folder. Click Start and then click your user name. In your user folder, you will see a folder named Contacts, and that is where Windows Vista stores your contacts. You can then copy the Contacts folder to a removable disk or other backup location.

E-mail an
ELECTRONIC BUSINESS CARD

You can create an electronic version of a business card that includes your name, address, and contact information. You can then attach this business card to your messages, enabling other people to easily add you to their address books.

The ritual exchange of business cards is a common sight at meetings, conferences, and cocktail parties. With the advent of e-mail, however, fewer people are meeting face-to-face, so there are fewer opportunities to swap cards. Fortunately, Windows Mail offers a feature that enables you to exchange business cards electronically.

An electronic business card is called a *vCard* and, just like its paper counterpart, it includes the person's name, address, phone numbers, and other contact information. If you have an item in the Contacts folder for yourself, you can use it to create a vCard, which you can then attach to your messages. The recipient can then view the attached card and easily add you to his or her address book. Similarly, you can view vCards that are sent to you and add the senders to your Windows Vista Contacts list.

CREATE YOUR ELECTRONIC BUSINESS CARD

1 In Windows Mail, click File.

2 Click New.

3 Click Contact.

The Properties dialog box appears.

4 In the First text box, type your first name.

5 In the Last text box, type your last name.

6 In the E-mail text box, type your e-mail address.

7 Click Add.

8 Use the Work tab to specify the other information you want in your electronic business card.

9 Click OK.

SEND YOUR ELECTRONIC BUSINESS CARD

 # 66

① In Windows Mail, click Contacts.

You can also click Tools and then Contacts or press Ctrl+Shift+C.

The Contacts window appears.

② Right-click your name.

③ Click Send Contact.

Windows Mail displays a new message window.

● Your electronic business card file is attached to the new message.

④ Type the recipient's address.

⑤ Type a subject.

⑥ Type a message.

⑦ Click Send.

Windows Mail sends the message with your electronic business card attached.

TIPS

Try This!

If you want your electronic business card to be sent with every message, click Tools, Options to open the Options dialog box, and then click the Compose tab. In the Business Cards group, click the Mail check box (☐ changes to ☑), click the drop-down arrow in the Mail list, and then click your name. Click OK.

Did You Know?

If you receive a message that includes a vCard, you can see the business card icon in the preview pane. Click the icon and then click Open to open the attached vCard file. To add the sender to your Contacts list, click Add to my contacts.

Change the location of your
MESSAGE STORE

You can change the hard drive location that Windows Mail uses to store the contents of your message folders. This is useful if you are running out of space on the current hard drive and need to move the messages to a disk with more free space.

Windows Mail stores the contents of your Inbox, Outbox, Sent Items, Deleted Items, Drafts, and Junk E-mail folders, as well as any new folders you create, in a special hard drive location called the *message store*. The size of the message store depends on a

number of factors, including how often you use e-mail, how many messages you save, how often you clean out your Deleted Items folder, and so on.

However, it is not unusual for the message store to consume dozens or even hundreds of megabytes of disk space. If you are running low on disk space and your computer has another hard drive with more free space, you can give your message store room to grow by moving it to the other disk.

① In Windows Mail, click Tools.

② Click Options.

The Options dialog box appears.

③ Click the Advanced tab.

④ Click Maintenance.

The Maintenance dialog box appears.

⑤ Click Store Folder.

The Store Location dialog box appears.

⑥ Click Change.

The Browse for Folder dialog box appears.

⑦ Click the folder you want to use as the new location.

⑧ Click OK.

⑨ Click OK.

Windows Mail tells you to restart the program to put the new store location into effect.

⑩ Click OK.

⑪ Click Close.

⑫ Click OK.

⑬ Click Close to shut down Windows Mail and then restart the program.

Windows Mail moves the message store.

Important!

To speed up the process of moving the message store, you can do some folder maintenance before performing these steps. For example, delete any messages you no longer want, including any messages in the Deleted Items folder. You can also delete any folders that you no longer use.

More Options!

Another way to save disk space with Windows Mail is to compact your folders to remove wasted space caused by message deletions. Follow steps **1** to **4** to display the Maintenance dialog box. Use the Compact the database on shutdown every X runs spin box to specify a relatively small number of runs, such as 10 or 20; the default is 100. Click Close and then click OK.

ACTIVATE THE SPELL CHECKER
to eliminate message errors

You can make your e-mail messages easier to read and more professional in appearance by using the Windows Mail built-in spell checker to catch and fix spelling errors.

Your e-mail writing is not as formal as the writing you do for reports, papers, memos, or other long-format documents. After all, e-mail has traditionally been a system designed for the exchange of short messages containing information, queries, or requests. However, the increasing popularity of e-mail now means that many people use it as a distribution medium for longer messages.

Whether you use e-mail for short notes or long essays, you can detract from your message if your text contains more than a few spelling errors. Sending a message riddled with spelling mistakes can also reflect poorly on you, whether the recipient is your boss, your colleagues, a customer, or a recruiter.

To ensure your message is received in its best light, you should activate the Windows Mail spell checker. This tool then checks your text for errors each time you send a message and it offers suggested replacements.

ACTIVATE THE SPELL CHECKER

① Click Tools.

② Click Options.

The Options dialog box appears.

③ Click the Spelling tab.

④ Click the Always check spelling before sending check box (☐ changes to ☑).

⑤ Click OK.

Windows Mail activates the spell checker.

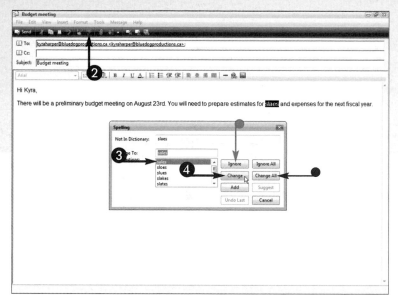

68

1 Start a new message and type the body text.

2 Click Spelling.

If Windows Mail finds a word that it does not recognize, it displays the Spelling dialog box.

3 Click the correction you want to use.

4 Click Change.

● If the word is correct, click Ignore to continue the spell check.

● If the mistake occurs multiple times in the message, click Change All, instead.

DIFFICULTY LEVEL

5 Repeat steps **3** and **4** for any other words flagged by the spell checker.

When the spell check is complete, Windows Mail displays a dialog box to let you know.

6 Click OK.

More Options!

The spell checker often flags a word that you know is correct. This can happen with people's names, company names and products, jargon terms, and so on. If Windows Mail flags such a word, you can prevent it from flagging the word in the future by clicking Add in the Spelling dialog box.

Customize It!

When you click Add, Windows Mail adds the word to a special file. If you have a number of names or jargon terms you want to add, you can edit this file directly. Press Windows Logo+R to open the Run dialog box and type **notepad %LocalAppData%\Microsoft\ Windows Mail\UserDictionary.lex** in the Open text box. Click OK and Windows Vista opens the file in Notepad. Add each word on a separate line.

CREATE A RULE QUICKLY
from a message

You can define a Windows Mail rule by creating the rule from an existing message. In Windows Mail, you use rules to examine incoming messages to set certain conditions. For example, if a message has a particular word or phrase in the Subject line or body, you can move the message to a special folder. Similarly, you can check for messages with attachments and elect not to download them from the mail server.

Perhaps the most common rule condition is to use the e-mail address of the sender. You can redirect

the message to a folder for that person's messages, send out an automatically reply, or even automatically delete the message if it comes from someone from whom you do not want to have contact.

With Windows Mail you can quickly define such rules by creating them from an existing message. In this case, Windows Mail automatically sets up the sender's e-mail address as a rule condition, so you need only define the action you want to perform on messages that come from that address.

① Click the message from which you want to create the rule.

② Click Message.

③ Click Create Rule From Message.

The New Mail Rule dialog box appears.

● Windows Mail automatically activates the Where the From line contains people condition.

● The sender's e-mail address appears in the Rule Description box.

④ Click an action to perform on messages from this address.

⑤ If the action requires more data, click the underlined placeholder.

Windows Mail displays a dialog box so you can specify a value for the placeholder. Note that the dialog box you see depends on the action you chose in step **4**.

6 Click the data (or, in some cases, type the text) to specify the placeholder value.

7 Click OK.

● Windows Mail fills in the placeholder value.

8 Type a name for the rule.

9 Click OK.

10 When Windows Mail tells you the rule was added, click OK.

TIPS

Apply It!

After you create the rule from the message, Windows Mail does not apply the rule right away. To apply the rule, click Tools, Message Rules, and then Mail. In the Message Rules dialog box, click Apply Now, click the rule you created, and then click Apply Now.

Remove It!

If you no longer require the rule, you can delete it. Click Tools, Message Rules, and then Mail to display the Message Rules dialog box. Click the rule and then click Remove. When Windows Mail asks you to confirm, click Yes.

SYNCHRONIZE A NEWSGROUP
to read posts offline

You can save connection time by synchronizing a newsgroup so that some or all of its posts are downloaded to your computer. You can then disconnect and read the posts at your leisure.

You can *synchronize* the newsgroup, which means that you download some or all of the newsgroup's data to your computer. You can disconnect from the Internet and read the newsgroup's post offline.

When you synchronize a newsgroup, you have three choices that govern the amount of information you download. The All Messages option means you

download every available message in the newsgroup, which is useful for newsgroups that have only a moderate number of messages. The New Messages Only option means you download only those messages that posted since the last time you synchronized. Finally, the Headers Only option means you download just the message headers — the sender's address and the Subject line — which is useful for newsgroups with a large number of messages. You can then select individual messages to download.

SYNCHRONIZE A NEWSGROUP

1 Click the newsgroup you want to synchronize.

2 Click Tools.

3 Click Synchronize Newsgroup.

The Synchronize Newsgroup dialog box appears.

4 Click the Get the following items check box (☐ changes to ☑).

5 Click the synchronization option you want to use (○ changes to ◉).

6 Click OK.

Windows Mail synchronizes the newsgroup.

⑦ If you chose the Headers Only synchronization, right-click a message that you want to download.

⑧ Click Download Message Later.

● If you want to download the message and all of its responses, click Download Conversation Later, instead.

⑨ Repeat steps **7** and **8** for all the other messages you want to download.

⑩ Follow steps **1** to **3** to display the Synchronize Newsgroup dialog box.

⑪ Click the Get messages marked for download check box (☐ changes to ☑).

⑫ Click OK.

Windows Mail downloads the marked messages.

TIPS

More Options!

If you find that Windows Mail always downloads the messages no matter what synchronization setting you use, click Tools and then Options to display the Options dialog box. Click the Read tab and then click the Automatically download message when viewing in the Preview Pane check box (☑ changes to ☐). Click OK.

More Options!

By default, Windows Mail downloads only 300 headers each time you synchronize a newsgroup. To increase this number, click Tools and then Options to display the Options dialog box. Click the Read tab and then use the Get *X* headers at a time spin box to set the number of headers to download. The maximum number is 1,000. Click OK.

IMPROVE A NEWSGROUP
by rating its posts

You can improve a newsgroup for other people by rating the newsgroup's post. Most newsgroups are busy places that are frequented by a wide range of people. Some posts are extremely informative, interesting, and some people routinely make meaningful contributions to the group. Other posts are not so useful, whether they are off-topic or part of the flame wars that erupt in most newsgroups.

Unfortunately, separating the good posts from the bad is a difficult task. After you spend time in a group, you learn who the competent users are and

which users are not worth reading. For every other post, however, there is no way to know in advance whether the content is worth your time to read it.

Windows Mail aims to reduce that uncertainty by enabling you to rate any post using a simple scale: Useful or Not Useful. By rating posts, you help others decide which posts to read and which to ignore. Note that to rate a post, you must have an account on the Microsoft Passport Network — for example, an MSN Hotmail account.

1 Click the newsgroup with which you want to work.

2 Click the post you want to rate.

3 Click Sign In.

The Sign in to Windows Mail dialog box appears.

4 Type your Microsoft Passport Network e-mail address.

5 Type your password.

6 Click Sign In.

Windows Mail signs you in to the Passport Network.

⑦ Click the Rate menu.

⑧ Click either Useful or Not Useful.

DIFFICULTY LEVEL

● Windows Mail applies the rating.

TIPS

More Options!

After you have completed rating a newsgroup's posts, remember that you are still signed on to your Passport account. If you do not want to remain logged on — for example, if you will be leaving your computer unattended for a while — you can disconnect from Passport. Click Tools and then click Microsoft Communities: Sign Out.

Check It Out!

The Microsoft Passport Network is a universal logon service that enables you to access a wide variety of Web sites by using a single logon: your MSN Hotmail address and a password. To learn more about the Microsoft Passport Network and to sign up for an account, see www.passport.net.

Enhance Your Computer's Security and Privacy

These days you may be used to thinking that threats to your computer-related security and privacy only come from the Internet. That is not surprising because the very real threats of e-mail viruses, system intruders, and identity thieves receive the lion's share of press coverage.

However, many security experts believe that most violations of security and privacy occur not remotely from the Internet, but locally, right at your computer. That is, computer security and privacy are comprised most often by someone simply sitting down at another person's machine while that person is not around. That makes some sense, because having physical access to a computer allows an intruder to install malicious programs, disable security features, and poke around for sensitive data, such as passwords and credit card numbers.

If you are worried about having your security or privacy compromised by someone having direct access to your computer, Windows Vista offers a reassuringly large number of tools and features that you can use to lock up your computer. In this chapter, you learn about most of these tools, many of which are quite simple to implement. Techniques such as adding a password to your account, putting your screen saver in security mode, and clearing your list of recently used documents and media files are all easy to set up, but provide greatly enhanced security and privacy. You also learn more advanced techniques that take security to the next level, including using advanced file permissions and preventing other people from even starting your computer.

Top 100

PROTECT A FILE OR FOLDER
with permissions

You can use file permissions to specify which users of your computer can access which folders, and what exactly those users can do with the files in those folders.

Windows Vista offers a sophisticated file security system called permissions. *Permissions* specify exactly what the groups or users can do with the contents of the protected folder. There are six types of permissions.

With **Full Control** permission, users can perform any of the actions listed. Users can also change permissions. With **Modify** permission, users can

view the folder contents, open files, edit files, create new files and subfolders, delete files, and run programs. With **Read and Execute** permission, users can view the folder contents, open files, and run programs. With **List Folder Contents** permission, users can view the folder contents. With **Read** permission, users can open files, but cannot edit them. Finally, with **Write** permission, users can create new files and subfolders and open and edit existing files.

In each case, you can either allow the permission or deny it.

❶ In a folder window, right-click the folder that you want to protect.

❷ Click Properties.

The folder's Properties dialog box appears.

❸ Click the Security tab.

● This Groups or user names list displays the current groups and users that have permissions for the folder.

Note: The name in parentheses takes the form COMPUTER\Name, where COMPUTER is the computer's name and Name is the user or group name.

❹ Click Edit.

❺ Click Add.

The Select Users or Groups dialog box appears.

6 Type the name of the group or user with whom you want to work.

7 Click OK.

● The user or group appears in this list.

8 Click the new user or group to select it.

9 In the Allow column, click each permission that you want to allow (☑) or disallow (☐).

10 Click OK.

11 Click OK.

Windows protects the folder with the permissions you selected.

TIPS

More Options!

In the Select Users or Groups dialog box, if you are not sure about a user or group name, click Advanced and then Find Now. Windows Vista displays a list of all the available users and groups. Click the name you want in the list and then click OK.

More Options!

You can override a user's group permissions by clicking the corresponding check boxes in the Deny column (☐ changes to ☑). For example, to prevent a member of the Administrators group from viewing the contents of your folder, click the List Folder Contents in the Deny column check box (☐ changes to ☑).

ADD A PASSWORD
to your user account

You can configure your Windows Vista user account with a password. Another person cannot log on to your account unless he or she knows the password.

Right out of the box, Windows Vista is not very secure. In most cases, when you start your computer, you are taken directly to the Windows Vista desktop. That may be convenient not only for you, but also for a system snoop who starts your machine while you are not around. With full access to the system, the snoop can install a virus, a Trojan

horse — a program that enables the hacker to control your computer from the Internet — or a program that monitors your keystrokes to grab your passwords. It is also easy for the intruder to root around in your files looking for sensitive information or even to trash your precious data.

The first and most important step towards preventing all of this is to protect your user account with a password.

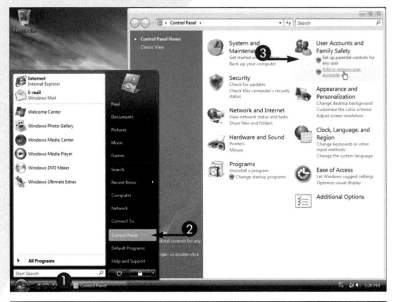

① Click Start.

② Click Control Panel.

The Control Panel window appears.

③ Click Add or remove user accounts.

Note: If the User Account Control dialog box appears, click Continue or type an administrator password and click Submit.

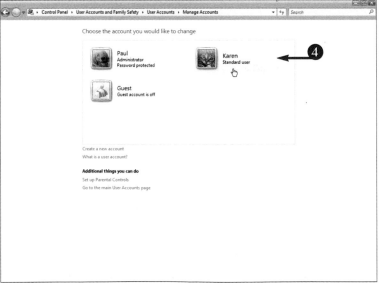

The Manage Accounts window appears.

④ Click the account to which you want to assign a password.

The Change an Account window appears.

5 Click Create a password.

The Create Password window appears.

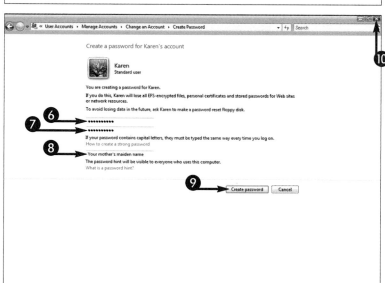

6 Type your password.

7 Type your password again.

8 Type a word or phrase as a hint.

9 Click Create password.

Windows adds the password to the account.

10 Click Close to shut down the Change an Account window.

Important!

When you choose a password, select one that nobody can guess, but one that you can remember. Here are some ideas:

● Do not use obvious passwords such as your name or your birth date.

● Use a password that is at least eight characters long.

● Do not write down your password.

● Do not tell your password to anyone.

Important!

Here are more ideas for creating a strong password:

● Because Windows Vista passwords are case-sensitive, mix uppercase and lowercase letters.

● Include numbers or punctuation marks in your password.

● Use a misspelled word.

● Use an acronym of a common phrase, such as the title of your favorite movie or book.

REQUIRE CTRL+ALT+DELETE
before logging on

You can configure Windows Vista to require users to press Ctrl+Alt+Delete before they can log on to your computer. This prevents a malicious program activated at startup from capturing your password.

Protecting your Windows Vista user account with a password (as described in Task #73), though an excellent idea, is not foolproof. Hackers are an endlessly resourceful bunch, and some of the smarter ones figured out a way to defeat the user account password system. The trick is that they install a virus or Trojan horse program — usually via an infected

e-mail message or malicious Web site — that loads itself when you start your computer. This program then displays a *fake* version of the Windows Vista Welcome screen. When you type your user name and password into this dialog box, the program records it and your system security is compromised.

To thwart this clever ruse, Windows Vista enables you to configure your system so that you must press Ctrl+Alt+Delete before you can log on. This key combination ensures that the authentic Welcome screen appears.

❶ Click Start.

❷ Click All Programs.

❸ Click Accessories.

❹ Click Run.

The Run dialog box appears.

❺ In the Open text box, type **control userpasswords2**.

❻ Click OK.

Note: If the User Account Control dialog box appears, click Continue or type an administrator password and click Submit.

The User Accounts dialog box appears.

7 Click the Users tab.

8 Click the Users must enter a user name and password to use this computer check box (☐ changes to ☑).

9 Click the Advanced tab.

10 Click Require users to press the Ctrl+Alt+Delete check box (☐ changes to ☑).

11 Click OK.

Windows now requires each user to press Ctrl+Alt+Delete to log on.

TIPS

Did You Know?

When you are logged on to Windows Vista, you can use Ctrl+Alt+Delete to change your user account password. Press Ctrl+Alt+Delete to display the Windows Security window, and then click Change a password. Type your old password, your new password (twice), press Enter, and then click OK.

More Options!

If you use the Run dialog box frequently, it can be a hassle to navigate the Start menus to launch it. One shortcut method is to hold down the Windows Logo key and press **R**. Alternatively, you can put the Run command on the main Start menu. Right-click Start, click Properties, click Customize, click the Run command check box (☐ changes to ☑), and click OK.

LOCK YOUR COMPUTER
to prevent others from using it

You can lock your computer to prevent another person from working with your computer while you are away from your desk.

Security measures such as advanced file permissions (Task #72) and encryption (Task #82) rely on the fact that you have entered the appropriate user name and password to log on to your Windows Vista account. In other words, after you log on, you become a "trusted" user.

But what happens when you leave your desk? If you remain logged on to Windows Vista, any other person who sits down at your computer can take advantage of your trusted-user status to view and work with secure files. You could prevent this by shutting down your computer every time you leave your desk, but that is not practical. A better solution is to lock your system before leaving your desk. Anyone who tries to use your computer must enter your password to access the Windows Vista desktop.

LOCK YOUR COMPUTER

❶ Click Start.

❷ Click Lock.

The Windows Vista Welcome screen appears.

● The word Locked appears below your user name.

UNLOCK YOUR COMPUTER

① Click inside the Password box.

② Type your password.

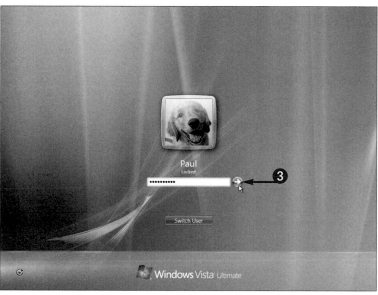

③ Click Go.

The Windows Vista desktop appears.

TIPS

Did You Know?

If you need to leave your desk in a hurry, Windows Vista offers a couple of quick ways to lock your computer. Perhaps the quickest way to lock your computer is to press the Windows Logo+L keys. Alternatively, press Ctrl+Alt+Delete and then click Lock Computer.

More Options!

Windows Vista also locks your computer when the screen saver kicks in. If this often happens while you are at your desk, you might want to turn off this feature. Click Start, Control Panel, Appearance and Personalization. Click Screen Saver, and then click the On resume, display logon screen check box (☑ changes to ☐). Click OK.

Prevent others from
STARTING YOUR COMPUTER

You can configure Windows Vista to require a special floppy disk to be inserted in your computer before starting up. Without the floppy disk, Windows Vista does not allow anyone to log on to the computer.

As a security feature, Windows Vista stores passwords in encrypted form. Vista uses a system key to decrypt the passwords. This system key is normally stored on your computer, and if for some reason the system key were lost, you would not be able to start your computer. For this reason, the system key is also called a startup key.

You can take advantage of this security precaution to make sure that no unauthorized user can start your computer. You do that by having Windows Vista move the startup key to a floppy disk. If the floppy disk is not inserted into the computer at startup, Windows Vista does not allow anyone to log on to the system. In fact, Windows Vista does not even display the Welcome screen, so an unauthorized user cannot even try to guess your password.

① Click Start.

② Click All Programs.

③ Click Accessories.

④ Right-click Command Prompt.

⑤ Click Run as administrator.

Note: If the User Account Control dialog box appears, click Continue or type an administrator password and click Submit.

The Command Prompt window appears.

⑥ Type **syskey**.

⑦ Press Enter.

⑧ Click Close to shut down the Command Prompt window.

168

The Securing the
Windows Account
Database dialog
box appears.

9 Click Update.

The Startup Key
dialog box appears.

10 Click the Store
Startup Key on
Floppy Disk option
(○ changes to ◉).

11 Click OK.

The Save Startup Key dialog box appears.

12 Insert a floppy disk into your computer's
floppy disk drive.

13 Click OK.

Windows Vista saves the startup key to the
floppy disk and then displays a
confirmation dialog box.

14 Click OK.

The Success dialog box appears.

15 Click OK.

Windows now requires the floppy disk
that contains the startup key to log on.

TIPS

Caution!

After saving the startup key to the floppy
disk, Windows Vista looks for the disk
when you start your computer. If Vista
does not find the key, the Windows Vista
Startup Key Disk dialog box appears. You
must insert the disk and then click OK.
If you lose or damage the disk, you
cannot start Windows Vista, so keep the
disk in a safe place. Also, be sure to make
a backup copy of the disk.

Remove It!

If you decide later on that you no longer
want to keep the startup key on a floppy
disk, you can revert to storing the key on
your computer. Follow steps **1** to **10**,
click the Store Startup Key Locally option
(○ changes to ◉), and then click OK.

HIDE RECENTLY USED DOCUMENTS
to enhance privacy

To enhance your privacy, you can clear the Start menu's Recent Items list and Media Player's list of recently played media files so that other people who use your computer cannot see which documents you have been working on.

The Start menu's Recent Items list is handy because it enables you to quickly open the last 15 documents you have worked on. However, if you know that someone else is going to be using your computer, and you do not have a separate user account set up for that person, you may not want him or her to see

what is on your Recent Items list. To prevent this, you can clear the list.

Windows Media Player maintains a list of files that you have played recently, and it also keeps track of the addresses of Internet media you have recently opened, as well as all the information you have downloaded about the audio CDs and DVDs you played. If someone else is going to use Windows Media Player on your computer, you can maintain your media privacy by clearing all this stored information.

CLEAR THE RECENT ITEMS LIST

① Click Start.

② Right-click Recent Items.

③ Click Clear Recent Items List.

● Windows Vista clears the My Recent Items List.

① In Windows Media Player, click the Now Playing menu.

② Click More Options.

The Options dialog box appears.

77

DIFFICULTY LEVEL

③ Click the Privacy tab.

④ Click Clear History to clear the list of recently viewed media files and Internet addresses.

⑤ Click Clear Caches to clear the downloaded information about audio CDs and DVDs.

⑥ Click OK.

Windows Media Player no longer lists your recently used media files or Internet addresses.

TIPS

More Options!

You can configure Windows Vista to never save recently used documents. Right-click Start, click Properties, and then click the Store and display a list of recently opened files check box (☑ changes to ☐). In the Media Player Privacy tab, click the Save file and URL history in the Player check box (☑ changes to ☐).

Did You Know?

The easiest way to maintain the privacy of your documents is to create separate user accounts for each person who uses your computer. Click Start, Control Panel, and then Add or remove user accounts. For maximum privacy, make everyone else a Standard user and assign a password to your account (see Task #73).

PREVENT MALICIOUS CODE
from running

You can prevent damage from some types of malicious programming by activating a feature that stops those programs from running code in protected portions of your computer's memory.

Windows Vista reserves some of your computer's memory as *system memory*, meant for use by Windows itself and by your programs. Windows reserves the rest of the memory for your open documents and other data. When programmers code software, they usually include fixed-size memory locations called *buffers* that hold data. Programs that require more data grab it from the hard drive and fill up the buffer.

Unfortunately, some poorly programmed software does not include a mechanism that watches for and prevents a *buffer overrun*: when a piece of data larger than the buffer size is loaded into the buffer. The extra data spills over into the system memory, resulting in system crashes. Some hackers use this flaw to deliberately crash or damage systems or even to run malicious code. Windows Vista includes a feature called Data Execution Prevention (DEP) that prevents buffer overruns, and so protects your computer from these attacks.

1 Click Start.

2 Right-click Computer.

3 Click Properties.

The System window appears.

4 Click Advanced System Settings.

Note: If the User Account Control dialog box appears, click Continue or type an administrator password and click Submit.

The System Properties dialog box appears.

5 Click the Advanced tab.

6 In the Performance group, click Settings.

The Performance Options dialog box appears.

7 Click the Data Execution Prevention tab.

8 Click the Turn on DEP for all program and services except those I select option (○ changes to ◉).

9 Click OK.

Windows Vista warns you that you must restart your computer to put the change into effect.

10 Click OK.

11 Click OK.

12 Restart your computer.

Windows applies Data Execution Prevention to all your programs.

TIPS

Important!

If Windows Vista detects a system memory intrusion, it shuts down the program that is causing the problem and displays an error message. You should immediately run a virus scan to ensure your computer is not infected. If there is no virus, the troublesome program may not work if DEP is turned on. Contact the software vendor to see if an updated version of the malfunctioning program is available.

More Options!

If you have trouble running a program when DEP is on, and your system is virus-free and no program update is available, you can turn off DEP for that program. Follow steps **1** to **8** and then click Add. Use the Open dialog box to display the program's folder, click the executable file that runs the program, and then click Open.

SWITCH TO ADVANCED SHARING

to improve security

If you share files with other network users, you can configure Windows Vista to control which users can access your files and what actions they can perform on those files.

If your computer is part of a network, it is common to give other users access to some of your files by sharing one or more folders with the network. By default, Windows Vista runs the Sharing Wizard when you opt to share a folder. The Sharing Wizard enables you to choose which users can share the

folder and how each person shares it: as a Co-owner (the user can make changes) or a Reader (the user cannot make changes).

If you want to apply more sophisticated sharing options such as the folder permissions discussed in Task #72, then you need to switch to Vista's advanced sharing features. These features enable you to set permissions for specific users and for groups of users (such as Administrators or Guests), create multiple shares for the same folder, and more.

① Click Start.

② Click Control Panel.

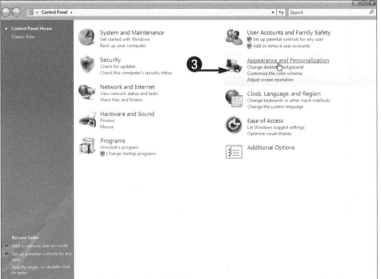

The Control Panel window appears.

③ Click Appearance and Personalization.

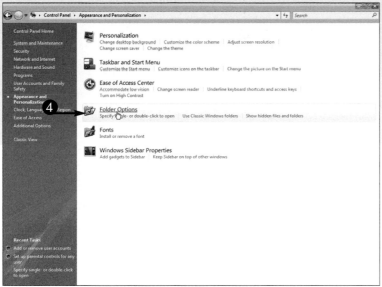

The Appearance and Personalization window appears.

④ Click Folder Options.

DIFFICULTY LEVEL

The Folder Options dialog box appears.

⑤ Click the View tab.

⑥ Click the Use Sharing Wizard check box (☑ changes to ☐).

⑦ Click OK.

Windows Vista switches to its advanced sharing options.

Did You Know?

If you have a folder window open, a quicker way to get to the Folder Options dialog box is to click Organize, then Folder and Search Options.

Did You Know?

To share a folder, click it, click Share, click the Sharing tab, and then click Advanced Sharing.

Important!

If your computer is part of a workgroup, you can set up an account for each user on every computer in the workgroup. For example, if the user Paul has an account on computer A, you must also set up an account for Paul on computers B, C, and so on. You must assign a password to the account and you must use the same password for the account on all the computers.

Safeguard your computer with a
SYSTEM IMAGE BACKUP

You can restore your system in the event of a major crash by performing a system image backup using the Windows Vista new Complete PC Backup feature.

Backing up your documents is important because a program crash, power failure, or imprudent deletion could cause one or more documents to be corrupted or lost.

However, PCs can also succumb to more major calamities, such as a virus or a hard drive failure. In such cases, you often lose access to your entire system. If you have just your documents backed up, you can restore them, but first you must reinstall all

your programs and devices, reconfigure Windows Vista, apply patches and security fixes, and perform other chores to get your system back to where it was.

A much easier road to recovery is to create a *system image backup*, which is a complete backup of your entire system. If you computer crashes, you can restore it to its previous configuration just by restoring the system image backup. Windows Vista enables you to perform such a backup by using its new Complete PC Backup feature, which is only available with Vista Business, Enterprise, and Ultimate.

❶ Click Start.

❷ Click All Programs.

❸ Click Accessories.

❹ Click System Tools.

❺ Click Backup Status and Configuration.

The Backup Status and Configuration window appears.

❻ Click Complete PC Backup.

❼ Click Create a backup now.

Note: *If the User Account Control dialog box appears, click Continue or type an administrator password and click Submit.*

The Where do you want to save the backup? dialog box appears.

8 If you want to back up to a hard disk, click the On a hard disk option (○ changes to ●) and use the list to click the hard disk you want to use.

● To back up to DVD discs, instead, click the On one or more DVDs option (○ changes to ●) and use the list to click the DVD burner you want to use.

9 Click Next.

The Please confirm your backup settings dialog box appears.

10 Click Start backup.

Windows Vista backs up your system.

TIPS

Important!

To perform a Complete PC backup to a hard drive, that drive must use the NTFS file system. To convert a drive to NTFS, click Start, All Programs, Accessories, right-click Command Prompt, and click Run as administrator. Type **convert *d*: /fs:ntfs**, where *d* is the letter of the hard drive you want to convert, and press Enter. If Windows Vista asks to "dismount the volume," press Y and then Enter.

Apply It!

If you need to restore you system, insert your Windows Vista disc, start your computer, wait for the message that prompts you to boot from the disc, and then press any key. When the Install Windows dialog box appears, click Next and then click System recovery options. Click Next, click Next again, and then click Complete PC Restore.

Allow a program through
WINDOWS FIREWALL

If you have a program that requires access to the Internet, you can prevent Windows Firewall from blocking it by setting it up as an exception.

Many programs require access to the Internet. For example, some programs have enhanced versions of their Help systems online at the developer's Web site and to use this content, the program must be able to connect to the Web site. Another common scenario is a program that checks online to see if an update is available and, if so, it downloads and installs that update.

Windows Firewall is a security program that Windows Vista uses to prevent unauthorized access to your computer. It blocks all programs from accessing the Internet, except those set up as exceptions. If you have a program that cannot access the Internet, then you can usually solve the problem by configuring that program as an exception to allow it through Windows Firewall.

Note that allowing a program through the firewall makes your computer a bit less secure, so you should only perform this task for programs that require Internet access.

① Click Start.

② Click Control Panel.

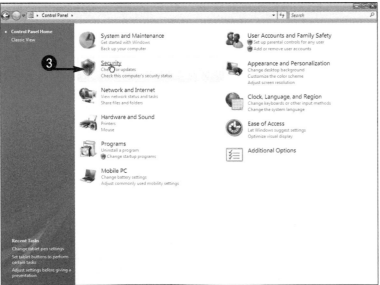

The Control Panel window appears.

③ Click Security.

The Security window appears.

④ Click Allow a program through Windows Firewall.

Note: *If the User Account Control dialog box appears, click Continue or type an administrator password and click Submit.*

The Windows Firewall dialog box appears.

⑤ Click the Exceptions tab.

⑥ If you see your program in the Program or service list, click the program (☐ changes to ☑).

⑦ If you do not see your program, click Add program.

⑧ Click the program.

⑨ Click OK.

⑩ Click OK.

TIPS

More Options!
In rare circumstances, a program requires access to the Internet via a specific port. (A *port* is an internal communications channel.) To allow this, follow steps **1** to **6**, and then click Add port to display the Add a Port dialog box. Type a name for the exception in the Name text box and type the port in the Port number text box. If the program uses the User Datagram Protocol, click the UDP option (◯ changes to ◉). Click OK.

Reverse It!
After you add a program to the Windows Firewall exceptions list, the program appears in the Exceptions tab with its check box activated. If the program no longer requires Internet access, you should disable its exception. Follow steps **1** to **6**, click the program (☑ changes to ☐), and then click OK.

ENCRYPT
confidential files and folders

You can encrypt your most sensitive and confidential files so that no other person can read them. Even if you have set up all the security mechanisms discussed in this chapter, it may still be possible for users to at least view your files. For example, hackers can use utilities to view the contents of your hard drive without logging on to Windows Vista. That is not so much of a problem if what you are worried about is other people altering or deleting your files. However, it is a very big problem if your computer has files that contain extremely sensitive or

confidential information: personal financial files, medical histories, corporate salary data, trade secrets, business plans, and journals or diaries.

If you are worried about anyone viewing these or other for-your-eyes-only files, Windows Vista enables you to *encrypt* the file information. Encryption encodes the file so that it is completely unreadable by anyone unless they log on to your Windows Vista account. After you encrypt your files, you work with them exactly as you did before, with no noticeable loss of performance.

1 In a folder window, click the folder containing the files that you want to encrypt.

Note: *You can encrypt individual files, but encrypting an entire folder is easier. That way, Windows Vista automatically encrypts new confidential files added to the folder.*

2 Click Organize.

3 Click Properties.

The folder's Properties dialog box appears.

4 Click the General tab.

5 Click Advanced.

The Advanced Attributes dialog box appears.

6 Click the Encrypt contents to secure data check box (☐ changes to ☑).

7 Click OK.

8 Click OK.

The Confirm Attribute Changes dialog box appears.

9 Click the Apply changes to this folder, subfolders and files option (◯ changes to ◉).

10 Click OK.

Windows Vista encrypts the folder's contents.

TIPS

Important!

To use file encryption, your hard drive must use NTFS (New Technology File System). To check the current file system, click Start then click Computer. In the Computer window, click the hard drive and then examine the File system information in the Details pane. If you need to convert a drive to NTFS, see the tip in Task #80.

More Options!

By default, Windows Vista displays the names of encrypted files and folders in a green font, which helps you to differentiate these items from unencrypted files and folders. If you would rather see encrypted file and folder names in the regular font, click Organize and then click Folder and Search Options. Click the View tab, click the Show encrypted or compressed NTFS files in color check box (☑ changes to ☐), and then click OK.

Get More Out of Your Notebook and Tablet PC

Windows Vista comes with many new features for notebook PCs and has support for Tablet PCs built-in to the operating system (except for the Home Basic edition of Windows Vista). If you use a notebook PC regularly, then you will appreciate Windows Vista features such as using an alarm to warn you when your battery power gets low, improving battery life with a custom power plan, and defining what action Windows Vista perform when you press the notebook's power buttons.

Windows Vista also enables you to set up your notebook with a special configuration to use whenever you use your notebook to give a presentation. For example, you can turn off your screen saver, mute the volume, and pick out a special desktop background.

For Tablet PCs, Windows Vista has many new features, including the following: support for pen flicks, which enable you to navigate a document and perform everyday chores with your digital pen; pen calibration to ensure accurate tapping; a program that lets you capture parts of the screen using your digital pen; the ability to insert handwritten characters automatically; and a system for improving the accuracy of Vista's handwriting recognition.

Top 100

SET A BATTERY ALARM
to avoid running out of power

You can configure Windows Vista to warn you when your notebook PC battery level is running low so that your computer does not shut down on you unexpectedly. If you are on a plane or in some other location where no AC outlet is available, you have no choice but to run your notebook PC on batteries. The ability to run on batteries is why notebooks are so convenient, but it has its downside: If your notebook batteries run out, you can lose your work.

To prevent this, you can configure Windows Vista to display a notification when the battery is low. This

warning gives you enough time to save your work and possibly shut down the computer until you can recharge it.

Windows Vista enables you to set the *low battery level*, which is the percentage of remaining battery life that triggers the alarm. The default low battery level is ten percent. If you opt for a lower value, you can also configure Windows Vista to automatically go to sleep or shut down when the low battery level is reached.

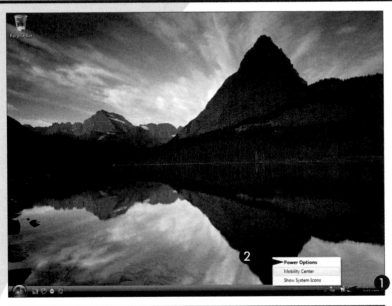

① Right-click the Power icon in the notification area.

② Click Power Options.

Note: *You can also double-click the Power icon.*

The Power Options window appears.

③ Click Change plan settings.

④ Click Change advanced power settings.

The Power Options dialog box appears.

⑤ Open the Battery branch.

⑥ Open Low battery level, click On battery, and type the percentage at which the low battery alarm triggers.

⑦ Open Low battery notification, click On battery, and click On.

⑧ Open Low battery action , click On battery, and click the action you want Windows Vista to take at the low battery level.

⑨ Click OK.

⑩ Click Save changes.

TIPS

More Options!

Windows Vista offers three different power plans: Balanced, High performance, and Power saver (see Task #84). You can set a lower power level and low power action for each power plan. Follow steps **1** to **4** to display the Power Options dialog box. Use the power plan list to click the power plan you want to customize, and then follow steps **5** to **9**.

More Options!

Windows Vista also supports a *critical battery level*, which triggers when your battery becomes dangerously low — the default level is five percent. When this level is triggered, Windows Vista immediately puts the computer into hibernate mode. To change this, follow steps **1** to **5**, open the Critical battery action branch, click On battery, and click the action you want. You can also open the Critical battery level branch to specify the critical level.

CREATE A CUSTOM POWER PLAN
to improve battery life

You can improve your notebook PC's battery life or increase your productivity by creating a custom power plan that suits the way you work.

When you use a notebook PC on battery power, you always have to choose between increased battery life and computer performance. For example, to increase battery life, Windows Vista shuts down components, such as the display and the hard disk after a short time. This reduces the performance of the notebook because you have to wait for these components to come back on again before you can return to work.

Conversely, to increase notebook performance, Windows Vista waits longer to shut down components. These two extremes are controlled by two of Windows Vista's predefined power plans: Power saver and High performance. The third power plan, Balanced, offers options that strike a balance between battery life and performance.

You may find that none of the predefined power plans is exactly right for you. If so, you can create a custom plan that suits your needs.

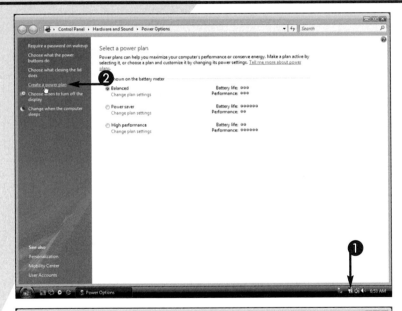

① Double-click the Power icon in the notification area.

The Power Options window appears.

② Click Create a power plan.

The Create a Power Plan window appears.

③ Click the predefined power plan to use as a starting point option (○ changes to ⊙).

④ Use the Plan name text box to type a name for your plan.

⑤ Click Next.

The Edit Plan Settings window appears.

6 Under On battery, use the Turn off the display list to click the idle interval after which Vista turns off the notebook's display.

7 Under On battery, use the Put the computer to sleep list to click the idle interval after which Vista puts the notebook into sleep mode.

8 Click Create.

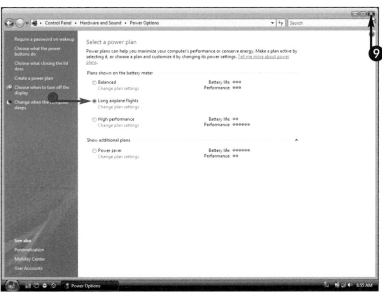

● The Power Options window appears with your custom plan displayed.

9 Click Close to shut down the Power Options window.

More Options!

To configure more advanced power options, such as when your hard disk powers down, open the Power Options window and click the Change plan settings link under your custom plan, and then click the Change advanced power settings link. In the Power Options dialog box, use branches, such as Hard disk, Sleep, and Processor power management to set the idle intervals. Click OK and then click Save changes.

Delete It!

To remove the custom plan, first change to a different plan by clicking the Power icon and then clicking another plan. Double-click the Power icon to open the Power Options window. Under your custom plan, click Change plan settings, and then click Delete this plan. When Windows Vista asks you to confirm, click OK.

Define actions for
NOTEBOOK POWER BUTTONS

You can get easy access to the Windows Vista notebook power down modes — shut down, sleep, and hibernate — by configuring your notebook's power buttons.

In shut down mode, Windows Vista closes your open programs and shuts off every computer component. The notebook uses no power while shut down.

In sleep mode, Windows Vista saves all open programs and documents to memory, and turns off everything but the memory chips. The notebook uses a bit of power (for the memory chips) while off. When you restart, Windows Vista restores your desktop as it was in just a few seconds.

In hibernate mode, Windows Vista saves your open programs and documents to a file, and then shuts down. The notebook uses no power while it is off. When you restart, Windows Vista restores your desktop from the file. This takes longer than in sleep mode, but less time than in shut down mode.

Most notebooks enable you to configure three "power buttons": the on/off button, the sleep button, and closing the lid. When you activate these buttons, they put your system into shut down, sleep, or hibernate mode.

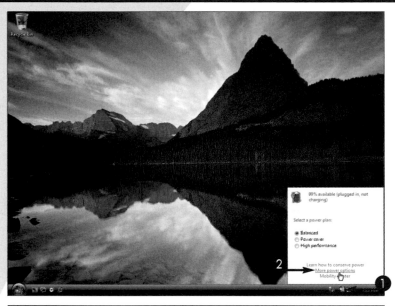

❶ Click the Power icon in the notification area.

❷ Click More power options.

Note: You can also double-click the Power icon.

The Power Options page appears.

❸ Click Choose what the power buttons do.

The System Settings window appears.

④ Under On battery, use the When I press the power button list to click Sleep, Hibernate, or Shut down.

⑤ Under On battery, use the When I press the sleep button list to click Do nothing, Sleep, or Hibernate.

⑥ Under On battery, use the When I close the lid list to click Do nothing, Sleep, Hibernate, or Shut down.

⑦ Repeat steps **3** to **5** for the lists in the Plugged in column.

⑧ Click Save changes.

Windows Vista puts the new power button settings into effect.

More Options!

By default, the options in the Password protection on wakeup section are disabled. This security feature forces Windows Vista to display the logon screen when your computer resumes from sleep or hibernate mode. If security is not a concern, you can enable the Don't require a password option by first clicking the Change settings that are currently unavailable link. If you see the User Account Control dialog box, click Continue or type an administrator's password and click Submit. You can now click Don't require a password (○ changes to ⦿).

Did You Know?

Many notebook computers do not come with a separate sleep button. On these computers, you usually simulate the sleep button by quickly tapping the machine's on/off button. Some keyboards come with a sleep key — it usually has an icon of a crescent moon — so if you have such a keyboard attached to your notebook you can enter sleep mode by pressing that key.

Adjust settings to
GIVE A BETTER PRESENTATION

If you use your notebook computer to make presentations, you can configure Windows Vista to use settings that ensure Vista does not interfere with your presentation.

When you give a presentation, your goal should be to have the audience focus on you and the material you are presenting. Unfortunately, if you use a notebook computer to show the presentation, it may interfere with that goal. For example, if your presentation is delayed while a discussion takes place, the computer might go to sleep or your screen saver might

activate. Similarly, your computer may display a notification that you have received a new e-mail message, or you may have a distracting desktop background image.

You can solve all of these problems by activating an option that tells Windows Vista you are currently giving a presentation. Windows Vista automatically keeps the computer awake and turns off system notifications. You can also configure Windows Vista to disable the screen saver and the desktop background while you are presenting.

❶ Click Start.

❷ Click Control Panel.

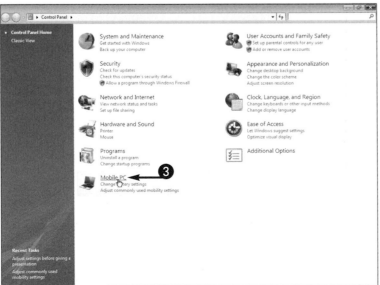

The Control Panel window appears.

❸ Click Mobile PC.

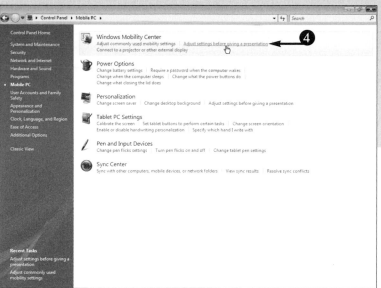

The Mobile PC window appears.

④ Click Adjust settings before giving a presentation.

The Presentation Settings dialog box appears.

#86

DIFFICULTY LEVEL

⑤ Click the I am currently giving a presentation check box (☐ changes to ☑).

⑥ Click the Turn off the screen saver check box (☐ changes to ☑).

⑦ If you want to set the presentation volume, click the Set the volume to check box (☐ changes to ☑) and click and drag the slider.

⑧ Click the Show this background check box (☐ changes to ☑).

⑨ Click None.

⑩ Click OK.

More Options!

Rather than disabling the desktop background, you may prefer to display a company logo or a photo of the product you are discussing. To display a background, follow steps **1** to **8**, click Browse, use the Browse dialog box to click the image you want to use, and then click Open. In the Position list, click Center, Tile, or Fit to Screen.

Important!

Windows Vista remembers your settings, so as along as you do not need to change your setup, in the future you can follow just steps **1** to **5** and then click OK. Note that each time you complete a presentation, you also need to follow just steps **1** to **5** to turn off the I am currently giving a presentation check box (☑ changes to ☐).

USE PEN FLICKS
to scroll and edit documents

If you are using your Tablet PC's digital pen, you can make it easier to navigate and edit documents by activating the Windows Vista new pen flicks option.

With a Tablet PC you can navigate a document either by using the Input Panel's on-screen keyboard or by using the program itself — for example, tap-and-dragging the vertical or horizontal scroll box or tapping the program's built-in navigation features.

Vista gives you a third choice for navigating a document: pen flicks. These are gestures that you can use in any application to scroll or navigate. To scroll up, move the pen straight up; to scroll down, move the pen straight down; to navigate backward in Internet Explorer or Windows Explorer, move the pen straight left; to navigate forward, move the pen straight right.

The pen flicks feature also supports the following editing gestures: Copy (move the pen up and to the left); Paste (up and to the right); Delete (down and to the right); and Undo (down and to the left).

1 Click Start.

2 Click Control Panel.

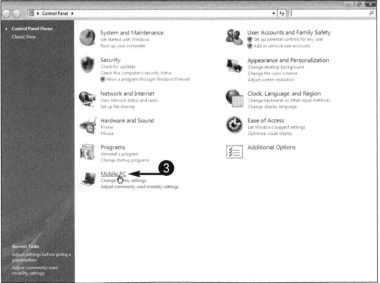

The Control Panel window appears.

3 Click Mobile PC.

The Mobile PC window appears.

④ Click Turn pen flicks on and off.

The Pen and Input Devices dialog box appears.

⑤ Click the Navigational flicks and editing flicks option (○ changes to ◉).

⑥ Click OK.

● After you perform your first pen flick, the Pen flicks icon appears in the taskbar's notification area. Click the icon to see a summary of the pen flicks gestures.

TIPS

More Options!

After you click the Navigational flicks and editing flicks option, the Customize button becomes active. Click Customize to display the Customize Flicks dialog box, which enables you to specify custom actions for the flick gestures. For each flick gesture, click its associated drop-down list and then click the action you want the gesture to perform. Click OK when you are done.

Important!

For a pen flick to work, you need to follow these techniques when performing the gesture: Move the pen across the screen for about half an inch (at least 10mm); move the pen very quickly; move the pen in a straight line; and lift your pen off the screen quickly at the end of the flick.

CALIBRATE THE TABLET PEN
for accurate tapping

You can make your Tablet PC digital pen easier to use by calibrating it with your screen.

It is likely that you mostly use your Tablet PC's digital pen for hand-writing characters using the Input Panel and hand-writing notes using a program such as Windows Journal. However, you can also use the digital pen in the same way that you would use your mouse. That is, you can tab an object to select it, double-tap an object to activate it, tap-and-drag an object to move it, and tap-and-hold an object to

display its shortcut menu (which is the pen equivalent of right-clicking the object).

These are all very handy gestures to know when you are using your digital pen. However, the usefulness of this feature declines if your digital pen is not calibrated to your Tablet PC screen. This can cause taps and double-taps to occur in places that are slightly off where you intended them to occur. This not only slows you down, but can cause errors. To prevent this, you need to calibrate your digital pen.

① Click Start.

② Click Control Panel.

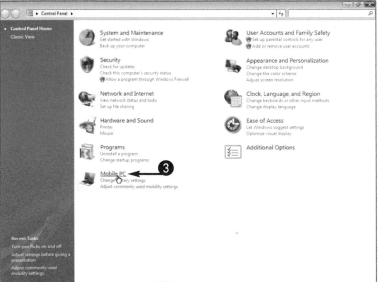

The Control Panel window appears.

③ Click Mobile PC.

The Mobile PC window appears.

④ Click Calibrate the screen.

The Tablet PC Settings dialog box appears.

⑤ Click Calibrate.

DIFFICULTY LEVEL

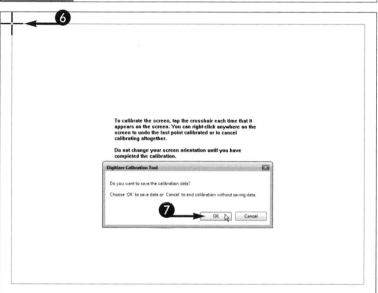

The calibration window appears.

⑥ Tap the middle of the crosshair each time it appears on your screen.

When the calibration is complete, the Digitizer Calibration Tool dialog box appears.

⑦ Click OK

⑧ In the Tablet PC Settings dialog box, click OK.

TIPS

More Options!

If you prefer to use the regular mouse pointer instead of the special pen cursor, you can turn off the pen cursor. Follow steps **1** to **3** to open the Mobile PC window, click Pen and Input Devices, click the Pointer Options tab, and then click Show pen cursors instead of mouse cursors when I use my pen (☑ changes to ☐). Click OK.

More Options!

If you tap the pen, Windows Vista displays an expanding circle at the tap position. If you find this kind of visual feedback distracting, you can turn it off. Follow steps **1** to **3** to open the Mobile PC window, click Pen and Input Devices, click the Pointer Options tab, and then click the check box for each action you no longer want visual feedback for (☑ changes to ☐). Click OK.

CAPTURE PART OF THE SCREEN
with the tablet pen

You can use the new Snipping Tool to capture part of the screen with your Tablet PC pen and save the result to an image file or Web page.

You can capture the current screen image by pressing the Print Screen key, opening Paint (or some other graphics program), and then running the Paste command to copy the screen image. An alternative is to press Alt+Print Screen to capture just the currently active window.

What if you just want to capture part of the screen? For example, you may want to show someone part of

a Web site or a dialog box. One solution would be use Print Screen to capture and paste the screen and then use your graphics program to crop the image to the section you want.

Windows Vista offers Tablet PC users (and also non-Tablet PC users) an easier method. It is called the Snipping Tool and it enables you to use your digital pen (or your mouse) to "draw" the area of the screen that you want to capture. You can then save the resulting "snip" as an image or an HTML file (Web page).

1 Display the image on screen that you want to capture.

2 Click Start.

3 Click All Programs.

4 Click Accessories.

5 Click Snipping Tool.

The Snipping Tool window appears.

6 Use your digital pen to draw the area of the screen that you want to capture.

A red line shows you the boundaries of the snip.

Note: The Snipping Tool window disappears temporarily from the screen as you draw the clip.

The Snipping Tool window appears and displays the snip.

7 Click Save Snip.

The Save As dialog box appears.

8 Use the File name text box to type a name for the snip file.

9 Use the Save as type list to click the file type you want to use.

10 Click Save.

● To save another snip, display the new object you want to capture, click New, and then follow steps **6** to **10**.

11 Click Close.

More Options!

If you want to share your snip with another person, you can send it via e-mail, which means you do not need to save it first. After you capture your snip, click File, click Send To, and then click E-mail Recipient. In the message window that appears, type the recipient's address in the To text box, type a Subject, and then click Send.

More Options!

You can annotate the snip before you save it or send it. To write text on the snip, click Tools, click Pen, and then click a pen color. Use your digital pen to write your text on the snip. If you want to highlight snip text, click Tools, click Highlighter, and then drag the digital pen across the text. You can also click Tools then Eraser to erase any annotations that you added.

Automatically insert
HANDWRITTEN CHARACTERS

You can perform your handwriting tasks more quickly by configuring the Input Panel to insert characters automatically after a specified time.

You will often use your Tablet PC's handwriting capabilities to create written notes in a program such as Windows Journal. However, you will usually want Windows Vista to convert your handwritten Input Panel text into computer text. For example, if you are entering an e-mail address in a message window, you can handwrite the address in the Input Panel and insert it as computer text that your e-mail program understands.

When you use the Input Panel's Writing Pad, you handwrite your text and then tap Insert to insert the computer text into the program you are using. Having to tap Insert is useful if Windows Vista does not always recognize your handwriting, because it gives you a chance to correct errors before inserting. However, if Vista accurately recognizes your handwriting, then you can have Vista insert your handwriting automatically.

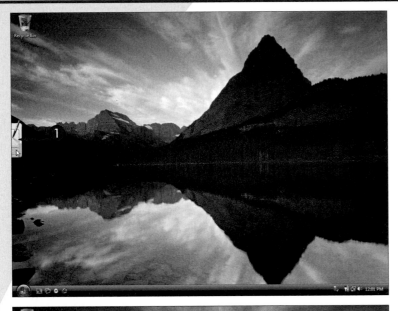

① Tap the Input Panel icon.

Windows Vista displays the Input Panel.

② Click Tools.

③ Click Options.

The Options dialog box appears.

④ Click the Writing Pad tab.

⑤ Click the Automatically insert individual characters after a pause check box (☐ changes to ☑).

⑥ Click and drag the Length of pause slider to set the interval after which Input Panel inserts the text.

⑦ Click OK.

Windows Vista puts the new settings into effect.

TIPS

Important!

The automatic insertion option only works for individual characters. You write a character, wait for it to be inserted, write the next character, and so on. If you choose a short insertion interval time, then you should not notice any delay when writing. If you want to temporarily stop the automatic insertion, quickly write two or more characters before the insertion interval is complete.

More Options

The Input Panel's Character Pad cannot insert characters automatically. However, you can make the Character Pad more efficient. In the Options dialog box, click the Settings tab and then, in the Insert button group, click the Left side of the writing area option (○ changes to ◉) and the Pointing to the Insert button inserts text option (○ changes to ◉).

IMPROVE HANDWRITING RECOGNITION
by enabling automatic learning

You can greatly improve the accuracy of Windows Vista's handwriting recognition by configuring Vista to automatically learn your handwriting style and your vocabulary.

You use the Input Panel to handwrite text for insertion as computer text. Also, programs such as Windows Journal enable you to handwrite notes and have them converted to computer text. However, the convenience and usefulness of handwritten text is directly related to how well the Vista recognition feature — called the *handwriting recognizer* — does its job. If it misinterprets too many characters, you

will spend too much time either correcting the errors or scratching out sections of text and starting again.

You can greatly improve the accuracy of the handwriting recognizer by configuring Windows Vista to learn how you handwrite text. This Automatic Learning feature does two things: it examines your handwriting style, and it keeps track of words you use in e-mail messages to increase the recognizer's dictionary. This data is stored on your PC and is not shared with Microsoft. However, you must activate this feature to take advantage of it.

① Click Start.

② Click Control Panel.

The Control Panel window appears.

③ Click Mobile PC.

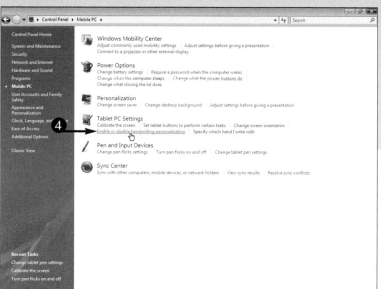

The Mobile PC window appears.

④ Click Enable or disable handwriting personalization.

91

DIFFICULTY LEVEL

⑤ Click the Use automatic learning option (○ changes to ⦿).

⑥ Click OK.

Windows Vista enables the Automatic Learning feature.

⑦ Click Close.

TIPS

Try This!

Windows Vista also comes with a personalized handwriting recognition tool that enables you to further improve the accuracy of the handwriting recognizer. Click Start, All Programs, Tablet PC, Personalize handwriting recognition. This displays the Handwriting Personalization window, which takes you through extensive exercises to target specific recognition errors and to teach the recognizer your handwriting style.

Did You Know?

You can help Microsoft improve its recognition software by sending them examples of the handwriting recognition errors you have corrected. Click Start, All Programs, Tablet PC, Report handwriting recognition errors. In the window that appears, click the check box beside each error that you want to report (☐ changes to ☑) and click Next. Click Accept for each correction, click Next, and then click Send.

Chapter 9: Get More Out of Your Notebook and Tablet PC

201

Maximize Windows Vista Networking

Most computers today do not operate in isolation. Instead, they are usually connected by one method or another to form a network. If you use your computer in a corporate or small business setting, then your network probably consists of computers wired together through devices such as hubs, switches, and routers. If you use your computer at home, then your network probably consists of computers connected wirelessly through a wireless access point.

Whatever the configuration of your network, it usually takes a bit of extra effort to get the

network working smoothly and to ensure that users can access network resources. The tasks in this chapter can help you get the most out of your network. You learn how to view the current network status; how to repair problems; how to customize your network name; how to share folders with other network users and how to protect those folders with advanced permissions; how to create a basic network between two computers with special devices such as hubs or access points; how to connect to a wireless network; and how to change the order of your wireless connections.

Top 100

VIEW THE CURRENT STATUS
of your network

You can make sure your network is operating at its most efficient by checking its current status from time to time.

These days, networks are generally quite reliable and you can often go for long periods without any problem. Of course, networks are not perfect, so slowdowns, outages, glitches, and other problems are bound to arise occasionally.

You can anticipate potential problems and gather network information in the event of a problem by viewing the network status. The status first tells you the most basic piece of information you require: whether the computer has a connection to the network. Beyond that, the status also tells you how long the computer has been connected to the network, how fast the network connection is and, for a wireless network, the strength of the wireless signal.

① Click Start.

② Click Control Panel.

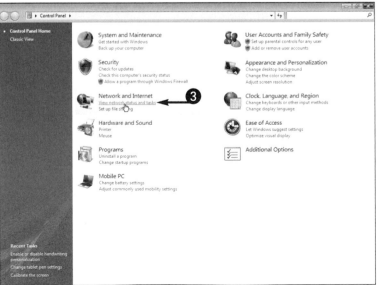

The Control Panel window appears.

③ Click View network status and tasks.

DIFFICULTY LEVEL

The Network and Sharing Center window appears.

● You can also open the Network and Sharing Center by clicking the Network icon and then clicking Network and Sharing Center.

④ Beside the network name, click View status.

The network connection's Status dialog box appears.

● The Duration tells you how long this computer has been connected to the network.

● The Speed tells you the current network connection speed.

● The Signal Strength tells you the strength of the wireless signal (the more green bars you see, the stronger the connection).

⑤ Click Close.

⑥ Click the Close box.

Did You Know?

It is not unusual these days for a computer to have multiple network connections. For example, you may have a wired connection with a couple of other computers at home, while also having a wireless connection to a gateway device that is connected to the Internet. In such cases, the Network and Sharing Center shows both connections: these are usually called Local Area Connection (wired) and Wireless Network Connection (wireless).

More Options!

On occasion you may need to know your computer's current IP (Internet Protocol) address, which is a unique value that identifies your computer on the network. To see your computer's current IP address, follow steps **1** to **4** to display the network connection's Status dialog box. Click Details to display the Network Connection Details dialog box, and then read the IPv4 Address value. Click Close.

RUN THE NETWORK DIAGNOSTICS TOOL
to repair problems

If you have trouble connecting to or accessing your network, Windows Vista comes with a diagnostics tool that can examine your network and then offer solutions. Networking in Windows Vista usually works quite well right out of the box. That is, you connect your computer to a wired or wireless network, and you can usually see other computers and work with their shared resources right away without the need for a complex configuration procedure.

However, despite the simple networking interface that Windows Vista presents to you, networks are

complex structures with many different hardware and software components working together. If just one of those components stops working or becomes unstable, you may encounter network problems. When network problems occur, tracking down and solving them is often quite difficult. Fortunately, Windows Vista comes with a tool called Windows Network Diagnostics that automates the process. It analyzes many different aspects of your network setup, and then offers solutions you can try.

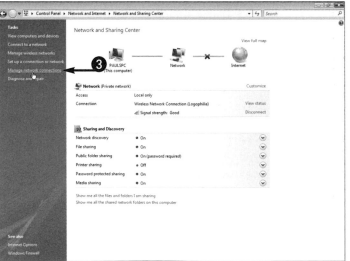

① Click the Network icon.

② Click Network and Sharing Center.

The Network and Sharing Center window appears.

③ Click Manage network connections.

The Network Connections window appears.

Windows Vista indicates the non-working network connection by adding a red X to the connection's icon.

4 Click the network connection that is not working.

5 Click Diagnose this connection.

The Windows Network Diagnostics dialog box appears.

6 Implement the solution suggested by Network Diagnostics.

7 Click the solution.

Note: *If the solution does not work, Network Diagnostics may suggest other solutions.*

● Windows tells you if the suggested solution works.

8 Click Close.

9 Click the Close box.

More Options!

Windows Vista supplies network connections with prosaic names such as Local Area Connection and Wireless Network Connection. If you would prefer to use names that are more meaningful or descriptive, you can rename your connections. Follow steps **1** to **3**, click the connection with which you want to work, and then click Rename this connection. Type the new name and press Enter.

More Options!

If you have multiple network adapters in your computer, Windows Vista sets up in the Network Connections window an icon for each adapter. You may need to test your network connections separately. The easiest way to do that is to disable all but one connection in the Network Connections window, and then run your tests. To disable a connection, follow steps **1** to **3**, click the connection you want to disable, and then click Disable this network device.

PERSONALIZE
your network name and icon

You can make the Network Center easier to navigate and you can help to differentiate between multiple networks by personalizing the network names and icons.

When you set up a network, Windows Vista gives the network a default name and icon that appear in the Network Center. The name is either a generic name such as Network or the default name that the network administrator has set up in a router or gateway device.

If you find yourself working in the Network Center window frequently, you may find the window easier to navigate if you assign more meaningful names to each network. This can also help you differentiate between networks.

1 Click the Network icon.

2 Click Network and Sharing Center.

The Network and Sharing Center window appears.

3 Click Customize.

The Set Network Location dialog box appears.

④ Use the Network text box to type the new network name.

⑤ Click Change.

The Change Network Icon dialog box appears.

⑥ Click the icon you want to use.

⑦ Click OK.

⑧ Click Next.

⑨ Click Close.

⑩ Click the Close box.

More Options!

To give yourself more choices when selecting a network icon, follow steps **1** to **5** to display the Change Network Icon dialog box. In the Look for icon in this file text box, type the following addresses (one at a time):

%SystemRoot%\system32\imageres.dll
%SystemRoot%\system32\shell32.dll

Important!

The Personalize Settings dialog box also displays the current category of the network. There are three categories: Private (used by home and small business networks), Public (used with networks available in public places such as coffee shops and airports), and Domain (used by corporate networks). Make sure your home or small business network is *not* set as Public. If it is, follow steps **1** to **3**, click Private, click Next, enter your credentials, and then click Close.

DISPLAY A NETWORK FOLDER
as a disk drive

You can gain easier access to a shared network folder by displaying the folder as though it were a disk drive on your computer.

You can use the Network window (click Start and then Network) to view the computers that are part of your network workgroup. If you want to work with a shared folder on one of these computers, you must open the computer that contains the folder, and then open the folder. If you want to work with a subfolder, you must also drill down through the subfolders until you get the one you want

This is not a big problem if you access network shares only rarely. However, navigating a number of folders every time you want to work with a shared resource is inefficient and time-consuming. To save time, Windows Vista enables you to display any shared network folder as though it were a disk drive on your computer. This is called *mapping* the network folder. The advantage of mapping is that an icon for the mapped folder appears in the Computer window (click Start and then Computer), so you can double-click the icon to access the folder.

❶ Click Start.

❷ Click Computer.

❸ Press Alt.

● The Classic menu bar appears.

❹ Click Tools.

❺ Click Map Network Drive.

The Map Network Drive dialog box appears.

6 Use the Drive list to click the drive letter you want to use for the mapped network folder.

7 Click Browse.

The Browse For Folder dialog box appears.

8 Click the network folder you want to use.

9 Click OK.

10 Click Finish.

 # 95

DIFFICULTY LEVEL

- Windows Vista opens a new window to display the contents of the mapped folder.

- An icon for the mapped folder appears in the Network Location section of the Computer window.

11 Click the Close box.

TIPS

Caution!
If you use a removable drive such as CompactFlash memory module, Windows Vista automatically assigns a drive letter to such a drive. This often causes a conflict if you have a mapped network folder that uses a lower drive letter (such as D, E, or F). Therefore, using higher drive letters (such as X, Y, and Z) for your mapped network folders is good practice.

Remove It!
To speed up the Windows Vista startup and reduce clutter in the Computer window, you can disconnect mapped network folders that you no longer use. To disconnect a mapped folder, click Start and then Computer. In the Network Location section, right-click the network drive you want to disconnect and then click Disconnect. If Windows Vista asks you to confirm, click Yes.

SHARE A FOLDER
with other users on the network

You can collaborate with other people on your network and allow users to work with some of your documents by sharing a folder with the network. The purpose of most networks is to share resources between the computers connected to the network. For example, the users on a network can share a single printer or an Internet connection.

This resource sharing also applies to documents. It might be a presentation that you want other people to comment on, a database with information that you

want others to use, or a worksheet that you want people to modify. In all these cases, the easiest way to give other people access to your documents is to share the document folder with the network. This task shows you how to set up basic folder sharing. See Task #97 to learn how to protect your shared folders with permissions.

To follow the steps in this task, you need to deactivate the Windows Vista Sharing Wizard. See Task #79 to learn how to deactivate this wizard.

① Open the folder that contains the folder you want to share.

② Right-click the folder you want to share.

③ Click Share.

● You can also click the Share button in the taskbar.

The folder's Properties dialog box appears.

④ Click Advanced Sharing.

Note: If the User Account Control dialog box appears, click Continue or type an administrator password and click Submit.

The Advanced Sharing dialog box appears.

⑤ Click the Share this folder check box (☐ changes to ☑).

⑥ Edit the Share name, if desired.

⑦ Click OK.

⑧ Click Close.

● Windows Vista adds the sharing icon to the shared folder's existing icon.

Note: If you do not see the sharing icon right away, press F5 to refresh the window.

⑨ Click the Close box.

TIPS

More Options!
If you want to change the share name of your folder, first follow steps **1** to **4** to display the Advanced Sharing dialog box. Click Add to display the New Share dialog box, type the new Share name you want to use, and click OK. Use the Share name list to click the old share name and then click Remove. Click OK and then click OK again.

Reverse It!
If you no longer want network users to access a folder, you can stop sharing it. Follow steps **1** to **4** to open the Advanced Sharing dialog box. Click the Share this folder check box (☑ changes to ☐). Click OK and then click Close.

PROTECT YOUR SHARED FOLDERS

with advanced file permissions

You can use file permissions to specify which network users can access which folders, and what exactly those users can do with the files in those folders.

In Task #72, you learned about using file permissions to control what other users on your computer can do with your files. Windows Vista offers a similar set of permissions for folders that you have shared with the network. Permissions specify exactly what specified users or groups can do with the contents of the protected network folder. In this case, there are three types of permissions.

With Full Control permission, network users can perform any of the actions listed. Network users can also change permissions. With Change permission, network users can view the folder contents, open files, edit files, create new files and subfolders, delete files, and run programs. With Read permission, network users can open files but cannot edit them.

In each case, you can either allow the permission or deny it.

① Follow steps **1** to **4** in Task #96 to open the Sharing dialog box.

② Click Permissions.

The folder's Permissions dialog box appears.

③ Click Add.

The Select Users or Groups dialog box appears.

④ Type the name of the group or user with which you want to work.

⑤ Click OK.

 # 97

DIFFICULTY LEVEL

● The user or group appears in this list.

⑥ Click the new user or group to select it.

⑦ In the Allow column, click each permission that you want to allow (☑) or disallow (☐).

⑧ Click OK.

⑨ Click OK.

⑩ Click OK.

Windows protects the folder with the permissions you selected.

TIPS

Caution!

By default, Windows Vista assigns Read permission to the Everyone group. This group represents every user or group that is not otherwise specified in the Permissions dialog box. For extra security, make sure you do not give the Everyone group Full Control or Change permission. If you only want your specified users and groups to access your shared folder, follow steps **1** and **2**, click Everyone, and then click Remove.

More Options!

By default, Windows Vista only allows people who have a user account on your computer — or people that know a user name and password on your computer — to access your shared folders. To change, click Start, Control Panel, and then Share files and folders. To change that, click the Network icon in the taskbar's notification area, and then click Network and Sharing Center. In the Sharing and Discovery section, click On beside the Password protected sharing item. Click Turn off password protected sharing (○ changes to ◉), click Apply, and then enter your credentials.

Work with
NETWORK FILES OFFLINE

You can work with network files and folders even when you are not connected to the network.

The benefit of using shared network folders is lost when you disconnect from the network. For example, suppose you have a notebook computer that you use to connect to the network while you are at the office. When you take the notebook on the road, you must disconnect from the network.

Fortunately, you can still get network access of a sort when you are disconnected from the network, or *offline*. Windows Vista has an Offline Files feature that enables you to preserve copies of network files

on your computer. You can then view and work with these files as though you were connected to the network.

When you reconnect to the network, Windows Vista automatically *synchronizes* the files. This means that Windows Vista does two things: First, it updates your offline files by creating copies of any new or changed files in the shared network folder. Second, it updates the shared network folder with the files you changed while you were offline. This synchronization occurs automatically when you log on to the network and when you log off the network.

① Click Start.

② Click Network.

The Network window appears.

③ Double-click the network computer with which you want to work.

The network computer's shared resources appear.

98

4 If the files you want to use offline are in a subfolder, open the folders until you see the subfolder you want.

5 Right-click the folder you want to use offline.

6 Click Always Available Offline.

DIFFICULTY LEVEL

Windows Vista makes local copies of the folder's files.

● The Always Available Offline dialog box appears.

7 Click Close.

Note: The Always Available Offline dialog box closes itself automatically after a few seconds.

● Windows Vista adds the Sync icon to the folder's regular icon.

You can now use the folder's files even when you are disconnected from the network.

TIPS

Did You Know?
You can also synchronize the offline files yourself. Follow steps **1** to **4** to display the shared network folder, open the folder, and then click the Sync button in the Task bar. If you have many offline folders to synchronize, click Start, Control Panel, Network and Internet, Sync Center, and then click Sync All.

Important!
When Windows Vista synchronizes your offline files, it may find that a file has been changed both on the network share and on your offline computer. In that case, the Sync Center reports that the "Sync failed" and displays a "conflict" link. Click that link, click the conflict, and then click Resolve. The Resolve Conflict dialog box gives you three options: keep the offline version of the file (you lose the network changes); keep the network version of the file (you lose your offline changes); or keep both versions (the offline version is saved under a modified filename).

Manually connect to a
HIDDEN WIRELESS NETWORK

If a nearby wireless network is not broadcasting its identity, you can still connect to that network by entering the connection settings manually.

Each wireless network has a network name — often called the Service Set Identifier, or SSID — that identifies the network to wireless devices and computers with wireless network cards. By default, most wireless networks broadcast the network name so that you can see the network and connect to it. However, some wireless networks disable network name broadcasting as a security precaution. The idea

behind this is that if an unauthorized user cannot see the network, he or she cannot attempt to connect to it. (However, some devices can pick up the network name when authorized computers connect to the network, so this is not a foolproof security measure.)

You can still connect to a hidden wireless network by entering the connection settings by hand. You need to know the network name, the network's security type and encryption type, and the network's security key or passphrase.

① Click Start.

② Click Connect To.

The Connect to a network window appears.

③ Click Set up a connection or network.

The Choose a connection option window appears.

④ Click Manually connect to a wireless network.

⑤ Click Next.

⑥ Type the Network name.

⑦ Use the Security type list to click the network's security type.

⑧ Use the Encryption type list to click the network's encryption type (if any).

⑨ Type the network's Security Key/Passphrase.

⑩ Click Next.

Windows Vista connects you to the network.

⑪ Click Close.

TIPS

More Options!

By default, Windows Vista activates the Start this connection automatically check box. This saves you from having to repeat the steps in this task each time you want to connect. However, Windows Vista may not connect automatically if the network is not broadcasting. To work around this, click the Connect even if the network is not broadcasting check box (☐ changes to ☑).

Caution!

Activating the Connect even if the network is not broadcasting check box could create a security problem for your network. The problem is that your computer will send out "probe" messages looking for the network if is not broadcasting. These messages include the name of the network. This is a security risk because a person with the right equipment can intercept those messages and learn the name of the hidden wireless network.

REORDER WIRELESS NETWORKS

to improve connections

You can change the order in which Windows Vista connects automatically to your wireless networks to ensure that you always connect first to the network you want. It is not unusual to have multiple wireless networks configured on your computer. For example, you may have two or more wireless gateways in your home or office. Windows Vista enables you to set up computer-to-computer wireless connections — called *ad hoc networks* — to share files or an Internet connection without going through a wireless access point.

By default, Windows Vista configures a wireless network with an automatic connection, so you get on the network as soon as Vista detects it. If you have multiple wireless networks, Windows Vista maintains a priority list, and a network higher in that list gets connected before a network lower in that list. If you are not getting connected to the wireless network you want, it may be that the network is lower on the network priority list. To work around this problem, you can move the network higher in the list.

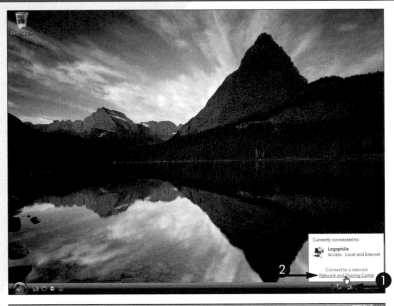

❶ Click the Network icon.

❷ Click Network and Sharing Center.

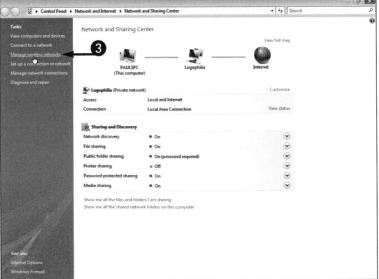

The Network and Sharing Center window appears.

❸ Click Manage wireless networks.

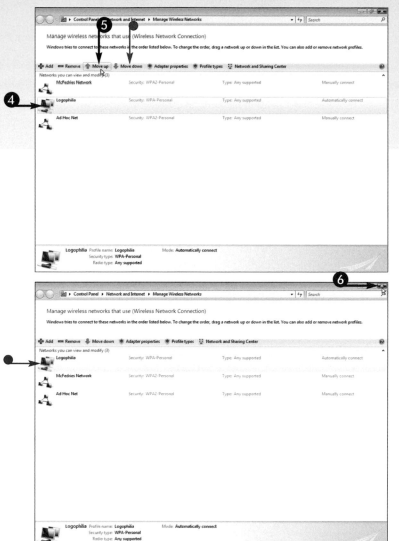

The Manage Wireless Networks window appears.

④ Click the network with which you want to work.

⑤ Click Move Up until the network is in the position you want.

● If you want to move a network down in the list, click Move Down, instead.

Note: You can also reorder the networks by clicking and dragging the network icons and dropping them in the position you want.

● Windows Vista reorders the networks.

⑥ Click the Close box.

TIPS

More Options!
You can also use the Manage Wireless Networks window to remove any wireless networks that you no longer use. Follow steps **1** to **3** to open the window. Click the network you want to delete and then click Remove. When Windows Vista asks you to confirm, click OK.

Try This!
If you want to try an ad hoc network between two Windows Vista computers, follow steps **1** to **3** to open the Manage Wireless Networks window. Click Add, click Create an ad hoc network, and click Next. Type a Network name, click WPA2-Personal in the Security type list, type a Security key between 8 and 63 characters long (the security key is case-sensitive), and click Next. After Windows Vista sets up the network, click Turn on Internet connection sharing, and then click Close.

Index

D

Data Execution Prevention (DEP), 172, 173
date, searching by, 82
default button, 34–35
default search provider, 129
DEP. *See* Data Execution Prevention
desktop shortcuts, 4–5
destinations, Send-To menu, 76–77
device drivers
    corrupted, 23
    rolling back, 25
    uninstalling, 25
    updating, 22–25
diagnostics tool, network, 206–207
digital pens. *See also* pen flicks
    calibrating, 194–195
    feedback on, 195
    screen capture with, 196–197
digital photos, repairing, 52–53
disk drive
    changing letter of, 42–43
    displaying network folder as, 210–211
    letter assignments for, 211
Documents folder, moving, 90–91
domain name, 107, 111
domain networks, 209
downloading media, 102–103
DPI Scaling dialog box, 45
drive letters, 42–43
drive space, 63

E

Ease of Access, 16–17
editing documents, 192–193
electronic business cards, 146–147
e-mail
    backup copy of contact list, 144–145
    Blocked Senders list, 106–107
    contact groups, 142–143
    country blocking, 108–109
    electronic business card, 146–147

    Junk E-mail folder, 104–105
    leave messages on server, 140
    location of message store, 148–149
    newsgroup rating posts, 156–157
    of screen capture, 197
    priority of messages, 141
    read receipts, 112–113
    rule creation, 152–153
    Safe Senders List, 110–111
    spam protection, 104–105
    spell checker, 150–151
    starting, 31
    synchronize newsgroups, 154–155
    virus protection, 114–115
encrypting files/folders, 180–181
enhanced content, 103
event tags, 56–57
Everyone group, 215
expanding groups, 89

F

file permissions, 160–161, 214–215
file properties, 80–81
file searches
    advanced, 80–83
    improving speed of, 14–15
    saving/reusing, 84–85
files
    add destination to Send-To menu, 76–77
    advanced file search, 80–83
    advanced sharing of, 174–175
    encrypting files, 180–181
    grouping/stacking, 88–89
    hiding, 170–171
    moving, 90–91
    offline network, 216–217
    opening, with programs, 74–75
    opening, with single-click, 72–73
    read-only protection, 78–79
    restore previous version of, 92–93
    searching. *See* file searches
    show/hide, 79
    sorting/filtering, 86–87

Index

filters
    file/folder, 86, 87
    Internet, 98–99
    pop-up ad, 136–137
    tagged image, 55

firewalls, 178–179

floppy disks, 168–169

folders. *See also* files
    add destination to Send-To menu, 76–77
    advanced file permissions for, 214–215
    advanced sharing of, 174–175
    displaying, as disk drive, 210–211
    drives as, 43
    encrypting files, 180–181
    moving, 90–91
    opening, with single-click, 72–73
    permissions used with, 160–161
    searching. *See* file searches
    sharing with other network users, 212–213
    sorting/filtering, 86–87

foreground programs, 8

Full Control permission, 160

Full Scan, 101

G

game ratings, 97

graphics memory, 7

green font (encrypted), 181

group permissions, 161

grouping files, 88

H

handwriting recognition, 200–201

handwritten characters, 198–199

hibernate mode, 188, 189

hiding documents, 170–171

home page, 122–123

HTML format, 114–115

I

icons
    large/small, 19
    network, 208–209

images
    categorizing, with tags, 54–55
    creating custom names for imported, 56–57
    repairing digital, 52–53
    rotating, 50–51

imported images, 56–57

Indexing Service catalog, 15

Internet Explorer
    browsing history deletion, 134–135
    links bar customization, 130–131
    open multiple pages on starting, 122–123
    pop-up ad viewing, 136–137
    Quick Tabs, 120–121
    saving Web sites, 132–133
    search engines, 128–129
    tabbed browsing, 118–119
    Web feed refresh frequency, 126–127
    Web feed subscription, 124–125

Internet Explorer Address Bar, 135

Internet Protocol (IP) address, 205

Internet security and privacy
    blocked senders list, 106–107
    country blocking, 108–109
    filtering, 98–99
    Media Player, 102–103
    parental controls, 96–97
    read receipts, 112–113
    safe senders list, 110–111
    spam protection, 104–105
    spyware, 100–101
    virus protection, 114–115

IP (Internet Protocol) address, 205

J

Junk E-mail folder, 104–105, 107

Index

Index